THE**NEOSOUL** GUITAR**BOOK**

A Complete Guide to Neo-Soul Guitar Style with Mark Lettieri

SIMON**PRATT**

KRISTOF**NEYENS**

MARK**LETTIERI**

FUNDAMENTAL**CHANGES**

The Neo-Soul Guitar Book

A Complete Guide to Neo-Soul Guitar Style with Mark Lettieri

Published by **www.fundamental-changes.com**

ISBN: 978-1-78933-017-5

Copyright © 2018 Simon Pratt and Kristof Neyens

Edited by Tim Pettingale

www.fundamental-changes.com

Twitter: **@guitar_joseph**

Over 10,000 fans on Facebook: **FundamentalChangesInGuitar**

Instagram: **FundamentalChanges**

For over 350 Free Guitar Lessons with Videos Check Out

www.fundamental-changes.com

Special thanks to Mark Lettieri for providing the tracks *Coastin'* and *Sunday Brunch* © Mark Lettieri

Cover Image Copyright: Taylor Guitars, used with permission.

Contents

Introduction

As a genre of popular music, Neo-Soul emerged in the late 1990s and was pioneered by artists such as D'Angelo, Jill Scott, Erykah Badu, Lauryn Hill and many more. The phrase "Neo-Soul" was coined by Kedar Massenburg of Motown Records, in order to distinguish the style from more conventional Soul and RnB.

When we discovered Neo-Soul we instantly fell in love. The combination of Gospel, RnB, Funk, Jazz and Hip-Hop, seamlessly blended all our favourite styles of guitar playing into one glorious sound. Now, several years on, being asked to write a book on the subject is a true honour.

In this book we will look at the important techniques, approaches and concepts that make up modern Neo-Soul guitar style, and break them down for you into a journey of over 100 musical examples, exercises and songs.

We're honoured to have worked with Mark Lettieri of the band Snarky Puppy for this book. Mark's style is infused with the influence of artists such as "Spanky" Alford, Jubu, Jonathan Dubose and Curtis Mayfield, to name a few, and we are thrilled that he has written two exclusive pieces for this book that you can learn in full. Not only that, Mark has recorded videos for each one so you can jam along with him.

If you've not heard much Neo-Soul before, it's essential to get its sound in your ears by doing some serious listening. By all means check out the artists we've mentioned thus far in order to understand where this music has come from, but in this book we are going to be referencing the guitarists we love who are the current torch bearers of the Neo-Soul flame. These are the players who are currently taking the genre to new places:

• Todd Pritchard

• Kerry "2Smooth" Marshall

• Landon Jordan

• Magnus Klausen

• Beau Diakowicz

• Isaiah Sharkey

• Curt Henderson

• Justus West

If you want to hear just three tracks that really capture today's Neo-Soul guitar sound, make sure to check out Montreal by Mark Lettieri, Movie by Tom Misch, and Nakamarra by Hiatus Kaiyote. This is Neo-Soul with a contemporary twist.

These tracks will lead you down a rabbit hole of musical discovery and get you well versed in the stylistic approaches of the genre. There are plenty of playlists on YouTube and time spent listening will massively improve your knowledge and understanding of Neo-Soul, and hopefully inspire you to give your all to the lessons in this book. Plus, it's fun and funky so you'll have a great time. You can thank us later!

This book is divided into two parts, the first dives straight in and breaks down the technical, chordal and single note approaches used by the greatest Neo-Soul players and condenses them into musical examples that you can use right away. When you apply these techniques to your own chord sequences and riffs, you'll quickly find your own unique style on the guitar.

All the techniques are taught around actual chord progressions you can use in your music instantly, so please feel free to steal our ideas.

The second part of this book begins in Chapter Seven and consists of four original Neo-Soul guitar tunes that have been specially commissioned for this book. Two pieces are by Mark Lettieri, along with a couple of pieces from us (Simon and Kristof). These tunes are designed to build your performance skills and teach you more musical applications of the techniques in Part One.

If you're new to Neo-Soul, we recommend that you work your way through this book from start to finish, so that you learn and develop the techniques in a logical fashion. If you've been playing Neo-Soul for a while and are just looking for some fresh ideas, feel free to jump in anywhere you like!

We believe in the value of having a "jam buddy" or a band to practise with, but fully understand this isn't possible for everyone. To help, we have included drum tracks and backing tracks to make the process of learning Neo-Soul as practical as possible. Refer to the end of the book, just before the conclusion, for more details on how to use these tracks.

Our hope for this book is that it will give you valuable tools to develop your Neo-Soul guitar skills or bust out of any ruts you may be in. It will definitely provide new challenges and insight as you seek to improve your playing.

It's also worth pointing out that, although highly suited to electric guitar playing, Neo-Soul also works well on acoustic guitar. we trust that you'll enjoy the book and expand your playing skills.

Happy Playing!

Simon and Kristof

Get the Audio

The audio files for this book are available to download for free from **www.fundamental-changes.com** and the link is in the top right corner of the site. Simply select this book title from the drop-down menu and follow the instructions to get the audio.

We recommend that you download the files directly to your computer, not to your tablet, and extract them there before adding them to your media library. You can then put them on your tablet, iPod or burn them to CD. There is a help PDF on the download page, and we provide technical support via the contact form.

Get the Videos

We've many tuition videos to go with this book, not least the two exclusive tracks by Mark Lettieri. Sometimes the limits of music notation doesn't quite do justice to the nuance of the music, so you should grab the videos for free from

https://www.fundamental-changes.com/neo-soul-videos/

Kindle / eReaders

To get the most out of this book, remember that you can double tap any image to enlarge it. Turn off 'column viewing' and hold your kindle in landscape mode.

Twitter: @guitar_joseph

Over 10,000 fans on Facebook: FundamentalChangesInGuitar

Instagram: FundamentalChanges

For over 350 Free Guitar Lessons with Videos Check Out

www.fundamental-changes.com

Chapter One – Chord Voicings and Embellishment

Artist spotlight: Todd Pritchard

One of the biggest misconceptions we've come across when teaching people Neo-Soul, is the belief that you need to be able to play complex chord voicings and extremely fast runs to sound authentic to the genre. In this chapter we dismantle this idea by showing you some fundamental voicings and grooves that encompass the Neo-Soul vibe, but are simple to grasp.

We first came across the concepts featured in this chapter while listening to Todd Pritchard. Todd is one of the most musical, grooviest players around. Check out his brilliant Instagram channel on the link below:

https://www.instagram.com/toddpritch/

After completing this chapter, you will not only have a strong grasp of essential chord shapes, but also understand how to apply them to a groove – a skill that is fundamental to the Neo-Soul sound. At the end of this chapter is an original piece by Simon entitled *Penguin Suit*, which features all the techniques illustrated in the examples.

A big part of the Neo-Soul sound is the use of 6th and 7th type chord voicings. Strum the three-note Emaj6 and Emaj7 voicings and hold them for four beats. Make sure you only play the designated strings.

Example 1a

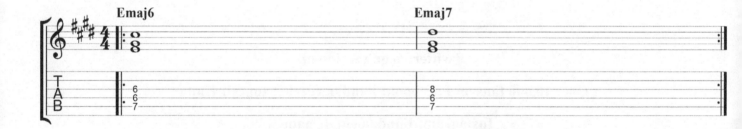

Often, fingerings are used whereby a 7th chord can easily be played with a hammer-on from a 6th chord. In Example 1b, barre the 6th fret and hammer-on your fourth finger at the 8th fret of the G string. Even by adding this simple hammer-on embellishment, you can instantly hear the basis of Neo-Soul patterns forming.

Example 1b

The combination of the movable Major 7 chord shape and the rhythmic pattern shown below is foundational to Neo-Soul. This concept is the backbone of many classic Neo-Soul tunes and will be built upon throughout this book.

Example 1c

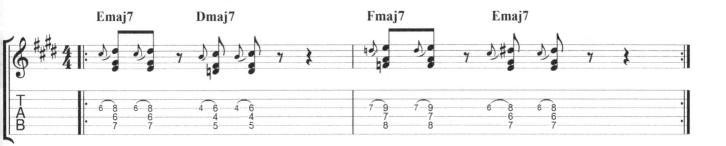

Neo-Soul relies heavily on the Major pentatonic scale. Example 1d adds a four-note E Major Pentatonic (E F# G# B C#) run to the end of a chord sequence. Use the E Major Pentatonic diagram below and play through Example 1d several times, using four different notes to end each time. Don't worry about which ones at first – experimentation is crucial. Write down your favourites in your practice journal.

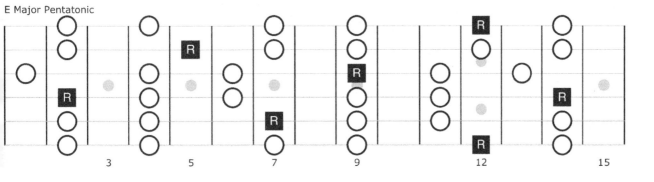

Example 1d

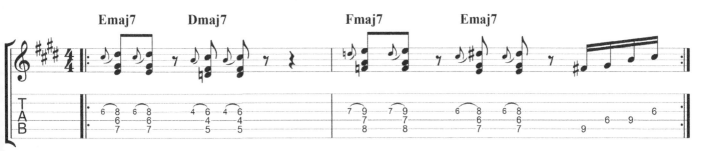

Combining small chord voicings with single-note melodic fills is a signature Neo-Soul sound, and vital to the construction of authentic sounding guitar parts. There are many ways to articulate single-note melodies, and adding a few slides will really liven up your playing. Example 1e adds a common slide to the Major 7 chord shape and moves the idea between EMaj7 and AMaj7. Example 1e is characteristic of Todd Pritchard's sound.

Example 1e

When you feel comfortable playing chord shapes on strings with the root note on the A string, let's dive into some ideas with the root note on the low E string. Play the three-note A6/9 and A6 chord shapes and hold them for four beats. If you are struggling to mute the A string, play the example using fingerpicking, or hybrid-picking (pick and fingers).

Example 1f

In Example 1g, play a hammer-on from the B to C# note on the G string while holding down the chord. By doing this you will alternate between an A6/9 chord and an A6 chord. Neo-Soul guitar parts often utilise a hammer-on or a pull-off to alternate chord shapes. Make sure the hammered-on note rings out as clearly as the notes of the E and D strings.

Example 1g

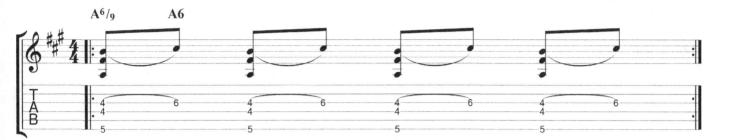

Example 1h combines the chord shapes learnt in the previous examples and includes Major 7th hammer-ons with a root on the A string, and Major 6 hammer-ons with a root on the E string. This is a fun mini-vamp to practise over example drum track 1.

Example 1h

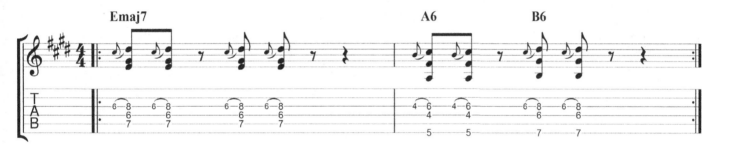

These three-note Cmaj7 and Am7 chord shapes, with a root note on the low E string, are extremely popular in Neo-Soul. You may be used to playing larger five- or six-note voicings for these shapes, but the voicings shown in Example 1i free up a finger for adding fills.

Example 1i

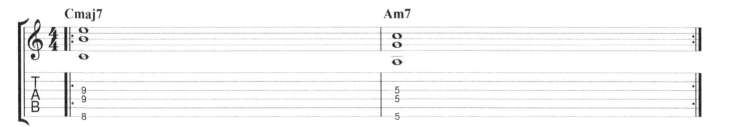

Example 1j introduces the chords and groove that will be used in the next few examples. Make sure you listen to how we phrase the examples by downloading the audio from **www.fundamental-changes.com**

Example 1j

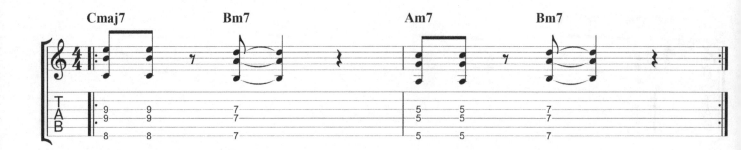

Example 1k adds hammer-ons and slides to the chords of the previous example, with double-stops (two-notes played at the same time) on the D and G strings. The double-stop notes played between each chord come from the G Major Pentatonic scale (G A B D E).

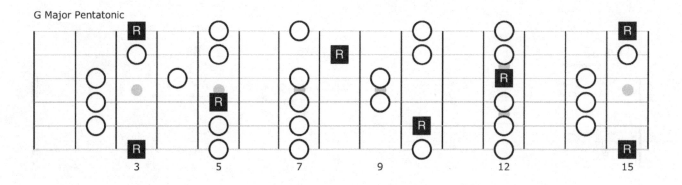

Example 1k

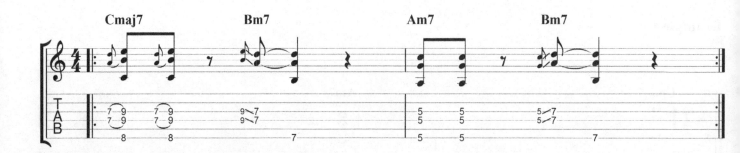

Let's extend the previous two-bar progression to make a four-bar progression that resolves to the key centre of G Major. Before moving on to the next examples, make sure you can play this progression by memory.

Example 1l

By adding in double-stops on the D and G strings from the G Major Pentatonic scale, the transitions between the chords begin to sound fluid and have that all-important Neo-Soul flavour. If you are looking for an extra challenge, experiment with adding percussive muted slaps where the rests appear in this example. To create a percussive mute, hit the strings lightly with the knuckles of your picking hand.

Example 1m

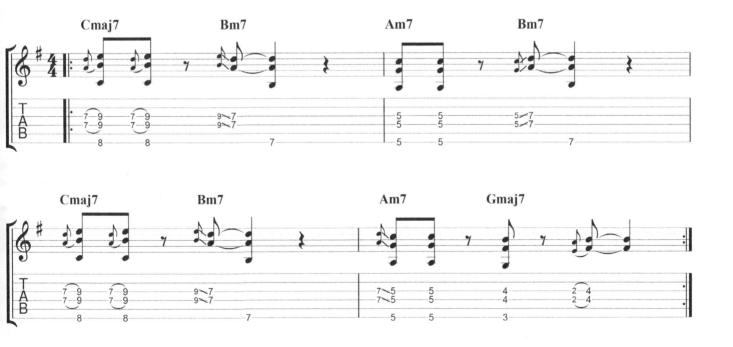

In this book, we want to give you as many ideas as possible to steal for your own playing, so along with the shorter examples, we have included some longer pieces for you to learn. The first of these tunes is by Simon and called *Penguin Suit*.

Before diving into the full piece, we have broken some of the main sections into bite-sized chunks. We recommend working through these examples before playing the piece in its entirety.

To master the specific fingerings, watch the *Penguin Suit* video **(https://www.fundamental-changes.com/neo-soul-videos/)**. You will notice that Simon fingerpicks this piece, but it works just as well when played with a pick.

Example 1n features the main "hook" of *Penguin Suit*. It is based around the D Major Scale (D E F# G A B C#). Practise each chord on its own before adding in the fills.

Example 1n

The B section of *Penguin Suit* uses chords voiced primarily with a sixth string root and adds slides and legato patterns between each one.

The double-stop sliding pattern at the end of bar two will require some extra attention to sound clean. There are a few ways to fret this, but we suggest using a first finger barre across the 2nd fret, and fretting the 4th and 5th frets with the third and fourth fingers respectively.

Example 1o

Example 1p teaches you the A Major scale lick that appears near the end of *Penguin Suit*. Notice how the combination of legato and slides give this lick its smooth, flowing sound.

Example 1p

The final run in the piece uses the E Major scale in multiple positions on the neck. If this type of run is new to you, we recommend learning it in bite-sized chunks before combining them. Learning just four notes of an unfamiliar pattern is a good place to start and you'll be surprised how much less daunting a longer phrase becomes if you break it up in this way.

Example 1q

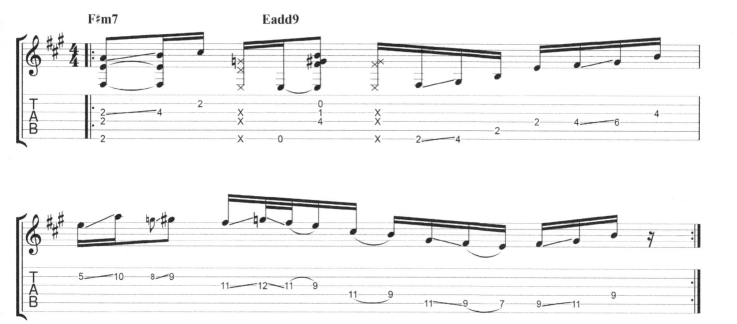

Now that you have completed the individual licks that make up this track, let's put them all together in the full version of *Penguin Suit*. Watch the video several times and listen closely to the phrasing of each part of the piece.

https://www.fundamental-changes.com/neo-soul-videos/

Penguin Suit - Full Piece

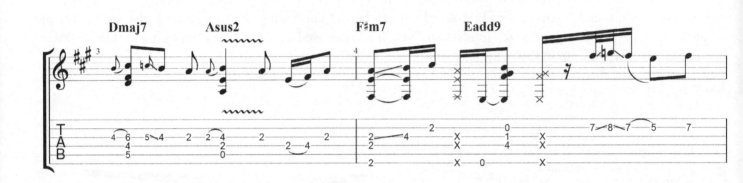

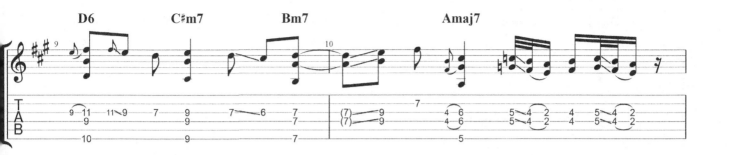

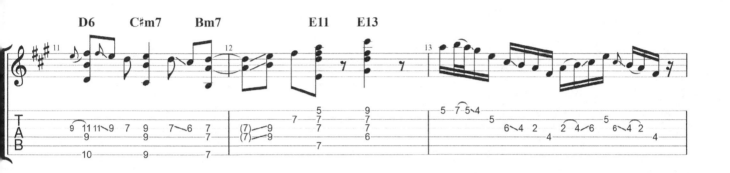

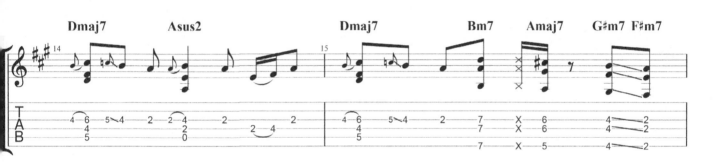

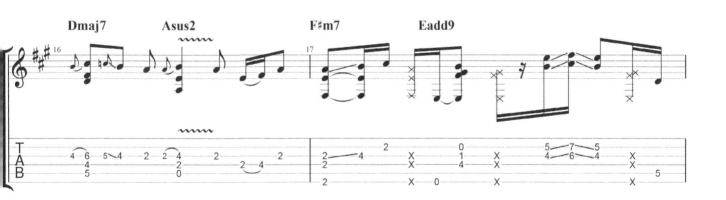

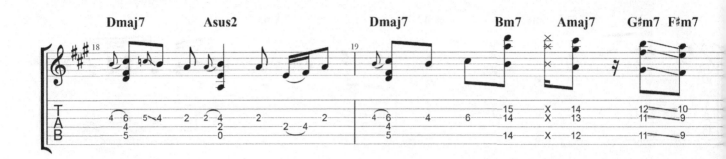

Chapter Two – RnB Chord Tricks

Artist Spotlight: Kerry "2Smooth" Marshall

Applying hammer-ons and pull-offs to barre chord shapes is a big part of the Neo-Soul guitar sound. These *legato* techniques have been borrowed from RnB, so we've named this chapter RnB Chord Tricks.

As teachers, we have both been asked countless times how to train the fourth finger to act independently while holding down barre chords, so in this chapter we've compiled our most effective exercises to help you develop the strength and independence needed in that finger. The first examples in this chapter are designed to teach you the essential techniques, but they will get more musical as you progress through the exercises.

If you are new to playing legato fills while holding down barre chord shapes, work through this chapter methodically and learn each example at 50 beats per minute. Don't be tempted to skip over the early examples in favour of applying this technique to chord shapes right away. Work through them methodically, as each example builds on the previous one in a structured fashion.

In Example 2a, hammer on between your first and fourth fingers on the B string. It is vital you use these specific fingers as this example is the foundation for all that follows.

Example 2a

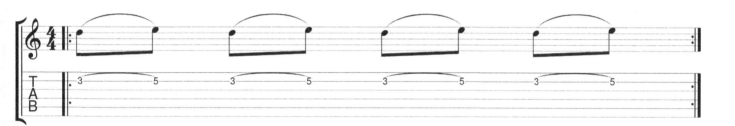

Now add a simple barre at the 3rd fret with your first finger and hammer-on to the 5th fret of the B string with your fourth finger. Make sure you push the barre shape down firmly and continue to hold the shape as you complete the hammer-on.

Example 2b

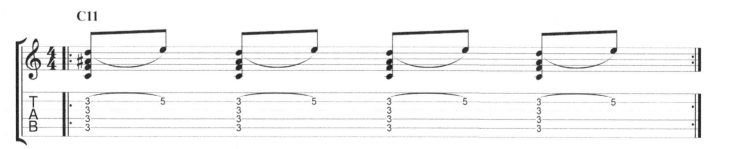

The next couple of examples use the more complex C Major 7th voicing shown in Example 2c.

Example 2c

Now that you have trained your fourth finger to act independently while holding a simple barre chord, let's apply that technique to the C Major 7. In Example 2d, play the Cmaj7 barre chord without the fourth finger, then hammer-on from the 3rd to the 5th fret on the B string.

Example 2d

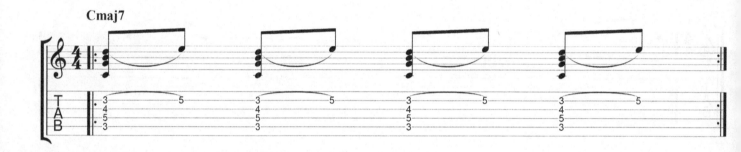

Example 2e introduces another common embellishment used in RnB chords. Complete the hammer-on pattern in exactly the same way as the previous example, but this time pick the note on the high E string afterwards.

As you progress through the examples in this chapter, take some time to listen to some examples of Kerry "2 Smooth" Marshall's playing. His approach to RnB chordal playing sums up everything you'll learn in this chapter. Here is a link to his awesome Instagram page:

https://www.instagram.com/kerry2smooth/

Example 2e

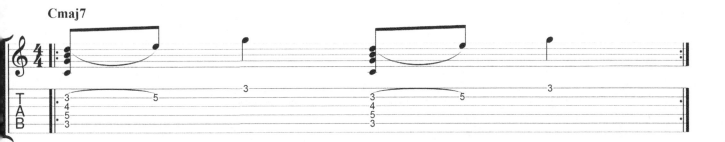

Another common adaption to the Major 7 barre chord shape in RnB is to create a hammer-on pattern on the high E string. In this case, it creates a Cmaj13 sound.

Example 2f

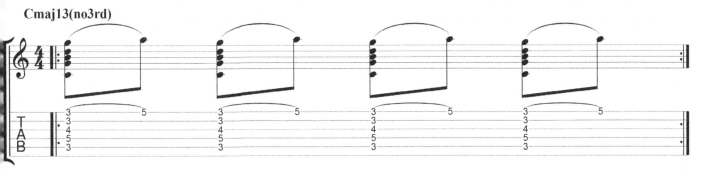

One of the many joys of the RnB chordal sound is the fluidity of the fills played around each chord. This is easily achieved by applying legato patterns on multiple strings. Example 2g combines the previously learnt legato patterns on the B and high E strings into one example. It really highlights the sound we are looking to create in this chapter.

To play Example 2g, use your fourth finger to complete the hammer-ons on both the B and E strings while continuing to hold the chord shape. Allow the chords to ring out as you complete each hammer-on.

Example 2g

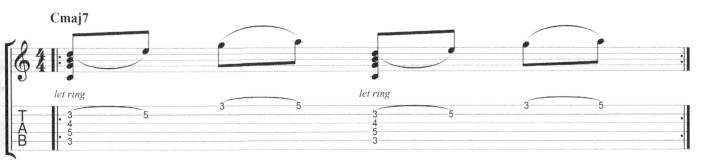

Now that you're comfortable hammering-on while holding down the Major 7 chord shape, it's time to add a pull-off. Play the pull-off from the fourth finger to the first finger, while still holding the barre. Make sure that all the notes sound clean and none are muted. This movement creates a Cmaj9 chord.

Example 2h

In Example 2i, pull off from the 5th to the 3rd fret of the high E string, from the fourth finger to the barred first finger. You may find the next couple of pull-off exercises trickier than the previous hammer-ons. This is perfectly normal! In time, with practice, they will feel just as comfortable as the hammer-ons.

Example 2i

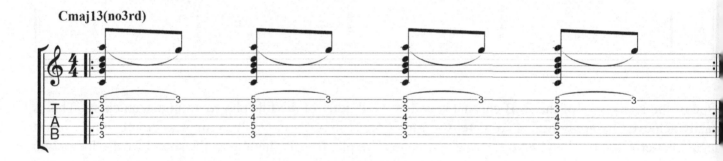

Until now we have concentrated on using 1/8th note patterns for each of the RnB style chordal licks. Example 2j features hammer-ons using the Major 7 chord shape, but this time uses 1/16th notes instead of 1/8th notes.

Example 2j

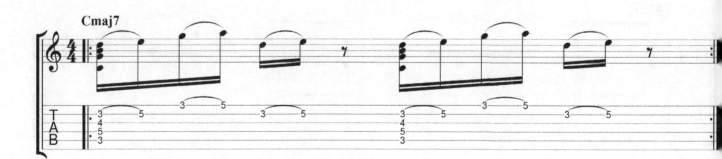

Practising hammer-ons and pull-offs separately is necessary to develop coordination, stamina and strength. The following example combines the hammer-on and pull-off patterns seen in previous examples into a commonly RnB chordal lick.

Example 2k

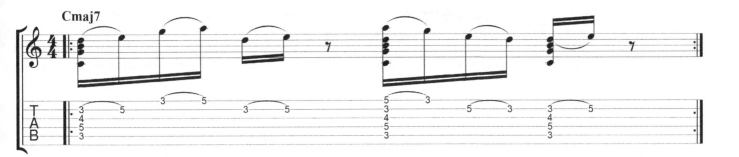

Now you have mastered common additions to the Major 7 shape, it's time to examine hammer-on and pull-off patterns around the Minor 7 chord shape.

Before completing the following examples, have a listen to this beautiful track by Kerry "2 Smooth" Marshall. See if you can recognise the chord shapes he is playing.

http://bit.ly/2REfFFn

In Example 2l, hammer-on from the 6th to the 8th fret of the B string using your second and fourth fingers. Make sure you stick to only using these fingers when completing this exercise, as they will be the only ones available when you apply it to the barre chord shape in the following examples.

Example 2l

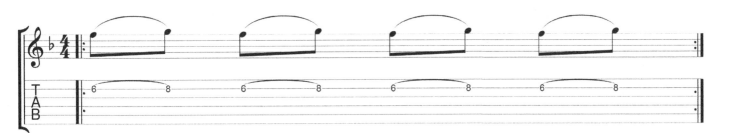

Now add this hammer-on pattern to a Dm7 chord shape with a root on the A string. Aim to make the hammered-on note ring out as clearly as possible by pressing the hammer-on firmly to the fretboard after you have strummed the chord shape.

Example 2m

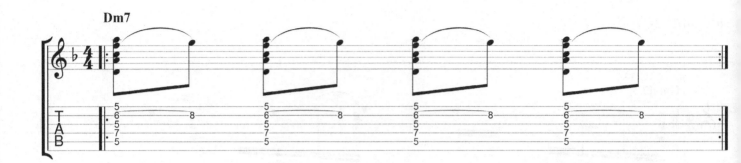

Another common adaption of the Minor 7 chord shape is to create a hammer-on pattern on the high E string. In this case we are in the key of D Minor, so we can use any of the notes of the D Minor Pentatonic scale (D F G A C) alongside the chord shape of Dm7. In Example 2n, hammer on from the 5th fret to the 8th fret of the high E string using your first and fourth fingers.

Example 2n

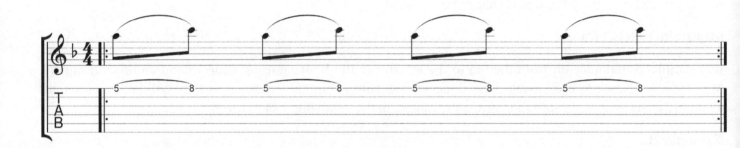

Now add the Dm7 chord shape to the previous hammer-on pattern.

Example 2o

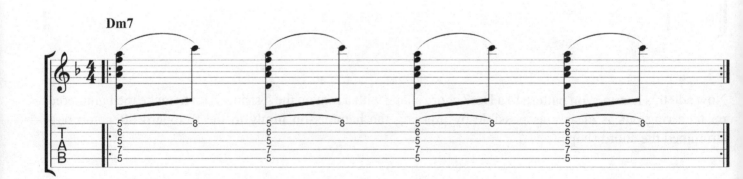

Combine the 6th to the 8th fret hammer-on pattern on the B string with the 5th to the 8th fret hammer-on pattern on the high E string. This is a brilliant warm-up exercise, as it combines both a barre chord shape and legato hammer-ons.

Example 2p

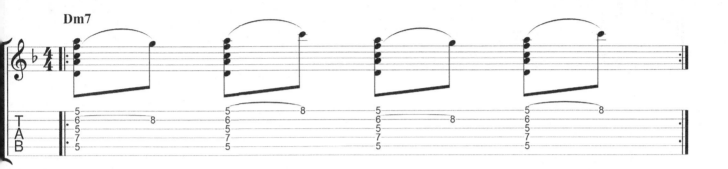

Once you have completed the hammer-on patterns around the Minor 7 chord shape, the next step is to practise pull-offs and hammer-ons together. If this kind of legato pattern is new to you, practise the pull-offs on their own before attempting Example 2q.

Example 2q

Now alternate between a Cmaj7 chord and a Dm7 chord using the legato patterns shown throughout this chapter. Things quickly start to get a bit more musical after all those exercises.

As you move through the next examples, be inspired by another Kerry "2 Smooth" piece from his Instagram.

http://bit.ly/2CaMww1

Example 2r

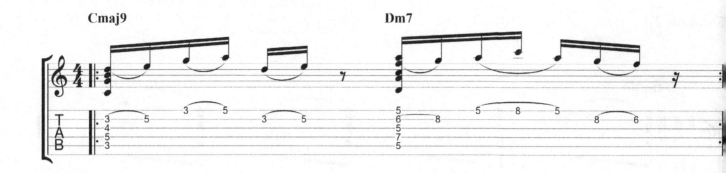

Example 2s is another great musical warm-up that combines multiple barre chords and legato. Start off slowly when learning this example, around 50 bpm, and make sure everything sounds clean before raising the tempo.

Example 2s

Chords with a root on the A string tend to be the most commonly used shapes in Neo-Soul, but it's important to play chord shapes in many positions on the neck. Example 2t shows a Minor 7 chord shape in the key of A Minor with the root on the E string. This is followed by a flurry of legato notes using the first and fourth fingers. To make learning these examples more fun, be sure to spend time playing them along with the backing tracks provided.

Example 2t

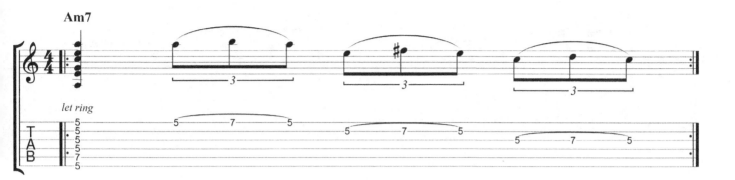

Now let's look at a Major 7 chord shape with the root note on the low E string and a frequently-used C Major scale legato fill.

Example 2u

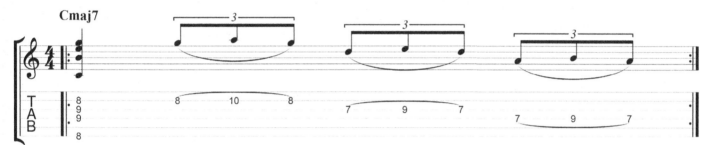

The final example of this chapter combines Major 7 and Minor 7 chord shapes on the low E and A strings with a variety of legato fills. As always, start off slowly and listen to the audio examples to see how each bar should be phrased.

Example 2v

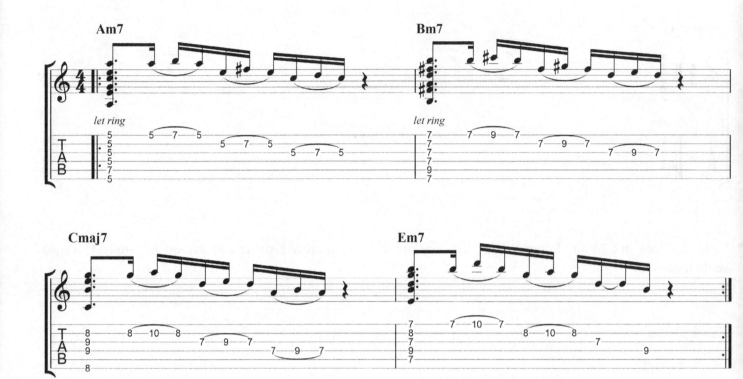

28

Chapter Three – Single Note Lines

Artist Spotlight: Landon Jordan, Magnus Klausen, Beau Diakowicz

Before we dive into this chapter, we want to introduce you to Landon Jordan. This young session player, based in Atlanta, demos products for companies such as Fender guitars. With his skills it's easy to see why he is one of the most sought after players around. Watch these magical eighteen seconds and enjoy the flow of single note lines with fluidity that is off the scale!

http://bit.ly/2NDSRCf

Another artist to check out is Magnus Klausen – a young Neo-Soul pioneer based in the UK. He has built a large Instagram following based on him blazing the way with fresh technical and melodic Neo-Soul ideas. Here is one of our favourite tracks of his. Note the crossover of jazz, blues, rock, gospel and other genres highlighted in this video.

http://bit.ly/2ITyWi2

By now you'll understand that a prominent feature of Neo-Soul guitar is the blend of beautiful jazz chord voicings and single note fills in between the chords. In this chapter we will break down some commonly used Neo-Soul fills – including pentatonic licks, arpeggios, chromatic passing tones and "outside" lines. Once you have absorbed the ideas in this chapter, use the concepts to create your own personalised approach.

Pentatonic ideas

The Major and Minor pentatonic scales are both popular choices among Neo-Soul guitarists. Using just five notes, these scales easily outline chord sounds and can fit into almost any playing situation. Legato techniques, such as slides, hammer-ons, pull-offs and grace notes are used to get the most out of each scale. Pay attention to how the techniques used influence the phrasing of each line and work to incorporate these ideas into your playing.

Example 3a uses the C Major Pentatonic scale (C D E G A) and has a gospel feel to it. This lick would work perfectly between the chords in any C Major progression, but is commonly played between Cmaj7 and Cmaj9 chords in Neo-Soul.

Example 3a

Example 3b contains three notes from the C Major Pentatonic scale played in three different octaves, and emphasises the importance of vibrato and slides. In the audio example you will hear this line played with a fast, subtle vibrato, but be sure to experiment with different speeds and amounts of vibrato.

This example shows how you can use different areas of the neck to create fills between your chords. For example, if you have three different Cmaj7 chords in a song you are creating, you could aim to write a fill in each of the different octaves shown in this example.

Example 3b

Example 3c uses the C Major Pentatonic scale to highlight the importance of short slides and hammer-ons.

Example 3c

One of the main differences between Neo-Soul and standard rock and blues is the heavy focus on Major chord progressions. In this chapter we've prioritised demonstrating Major pentatonic licks, as these will likely feel less familiar to you than their Minor counterparts.

The final Major Pentatonic lick moves away from C Major to the A Major Pentatonic scale (A B C# E F#).

Example 3d

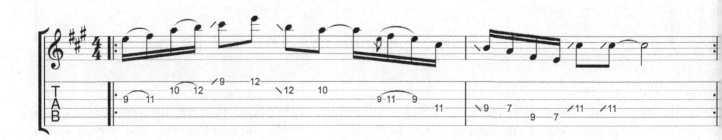

Arpeggio ideas

Neo-Soul single note lines rely on being smooth and fluid, and often use a lot of the fretboard to accomplish this. Arpeggios are a great navigational tool to move around the neck and in this section we'll look at the three most commonly used arpeggios used in Neo-Soul – Major 9, Minor 9 and Dominant 9.

When playing these lines, although you can pick each note separately, we have included specific legato passages which will help you create a flowing sound. These arpeggios are commonly played between chords and as fills when a longer run is required.

Before you play the arpeggios, we want to introduce you the phenomenon that is Beau Diakowicz. Truly, when we first came across him we were literally blown away. Check out this Soundslice lick from him and see how he uses arpeggios in bars five and seven to effortlessly move around the neck.

http://bit.ly/2A6zDSv

The most important thing you can do with the arpeggio patterns that follow is commit them to memory, not just read them off the page. This will take time, but the effort invested will be richly rewarded with long, beautiful lines that stun an audience.

At the end of each arpeggio we have included a chord voicing that you can play the arpeggio shape over. Use a loop pedal, a sequencer, or your phone to record the chord, then play the corresponding arpeggio shape over it.

Example 3e – Amaj9 Arpeggio

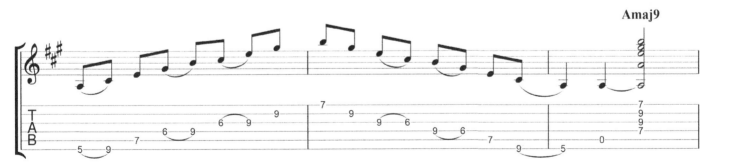

Example 3f – A9 Arpeggio

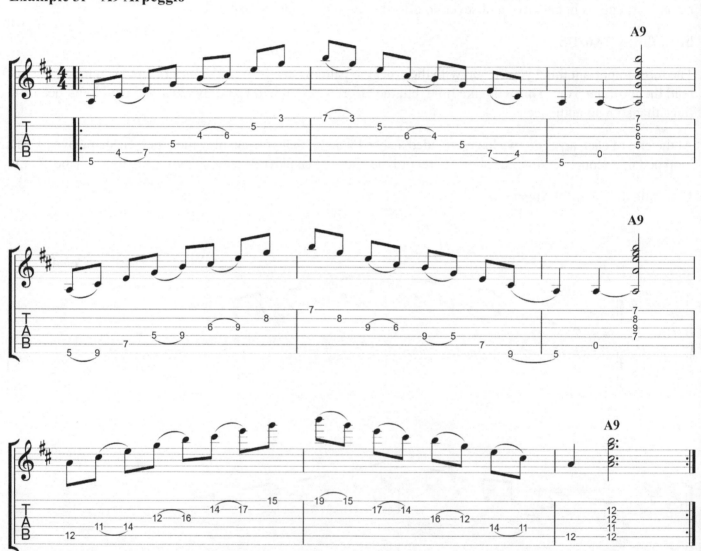

Example 3g – Am9 Arpeggio

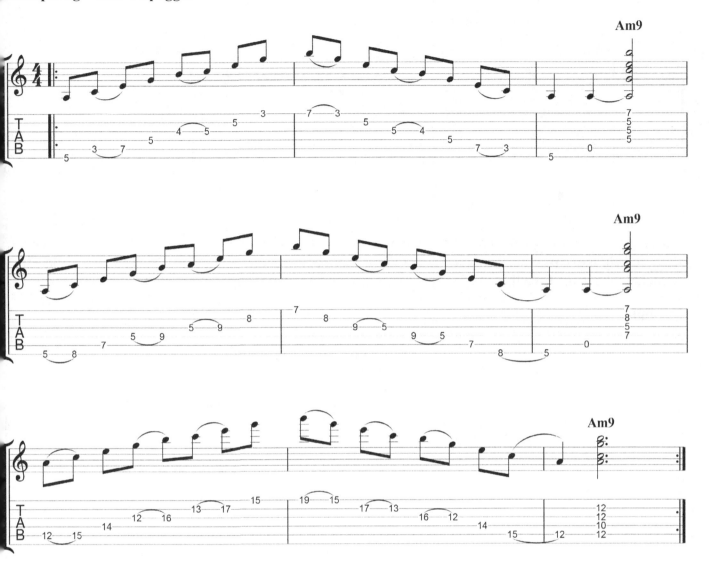

Example 3h demonstrates an Asus2 chord followed by an Amaj9 arpeggio (A C# E G# B) played with the notes re-arranged to create a lick. Make sure the arpeggio sounds smooth and let the notes ring to outline the Amaj9 chord. You can use this lick on any A Major chord, but in Neo-Soul that will commonly be Amaj7, Amaj9 or Aadd9.

Example 3h

Building on the previous example, Example 3i demonstrates an Em9 arpeggio (E G B D F#) that include
slides to help move position. Complete the slides with your first finger throughout this exercise. A fun way t
get double the value from these licks is to start at the end and play the lick in reverse.

Example 3i

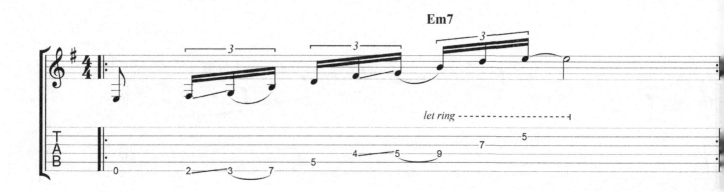

Example 3j demonstrates a nice way of connecting a Cmaj7 arpeggio (C E G B) to an Fmaj7 arpeggio (F A C
E). These arpeggio shapes are formed into fills that can be used between chords. Pay special attention to th
use of slides and hammer-ons throughout this example as they give it its unique sound.

Example 3j

So far we have concentrated on ascending fills and licks. Example 3k demonstrates a descending lick that uses the B Natural Minor scale (B C# D E F# G A) and ends with a popular Neo-Soul chord voicing. The flowing nature of this lick means it would work well after a B Minor chord voicing, such as Bm7 or Bm9. It could also work very well as the ending to a Neo-Soul piece.

Example 3k

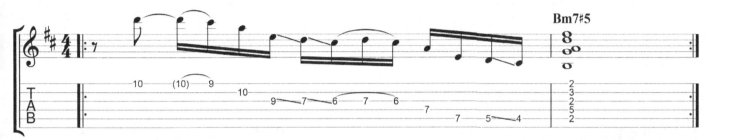

One of the main aims of this book is to teach you to be able to combine fills, licks and chords in a confident manner. As the Major 9 chord shape is so common in Neo-Soul, it is a good place to start when getting used to adding fills to your chord voicings. Example 3l starts off with a Bmaj9 voicing with the root on the A string, then uses the B Major scale with tiny slides, hammer-ons and pull-offs to define the feel of the lick.

Example 3l

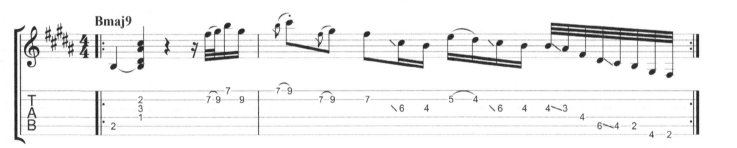

Example 3m uses the E Major Scale (E F# G# A B C# D#) to create a slippery fill that would work well over an E Major type chord, such as Emaj7 or Emaj9.

Take a look at the E Major Scale neck diagram below. When you are learning this example, pay special attention to the notes used in the lick that *do not* appear in the diagram. These passing notes have been added to create a sense of tension and release, and are not held for long.

E Major Scale

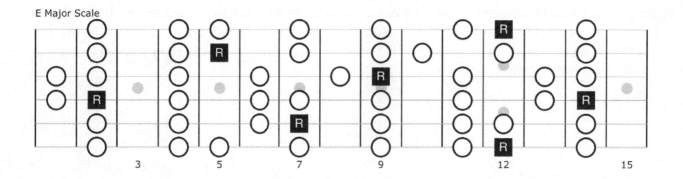

Example 3m

Practise the following E Natural Minor (E F# G A B C D) lick extremely slowly at first, *without* a metronome. The first two bars loop perfectly and work well as an all-finger legato warm-up. This lick works as a longer fill over any E Minor chord type. In Neo-Soul that will commonly be either Em7 or Em9.

When learning this example we recommend that you break the lick up into small chunks of three to four notes at a time. This will help you learn the lick quickly, but you can also use the mini phrases as licks in their own right, to use for shorter fills.

Example 3n

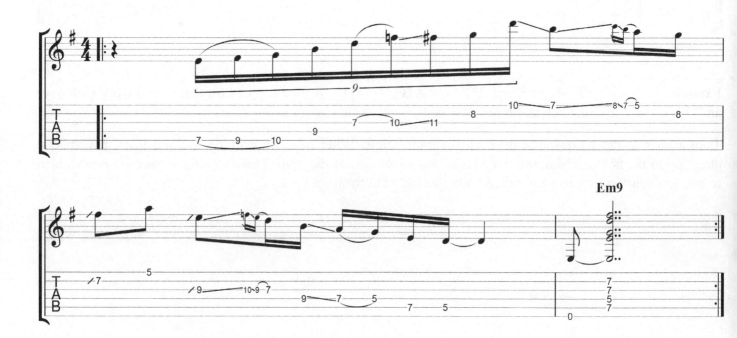

We call this next E Natural Minor lick the "slip and slide" as it really demonstrates the power of multiple slides joined together in a Neo-Soul context. This lick works fantastically over any E Minor chord. The Em11 chord featured in the second half of bar two should be held down as a full chord shape before applying the necessary hammer-on and slide.

Example 3o

A common way to create single note lines is to play using only one string. This can help you to break out of the conventional guitar box shapes and patterns. It also creates a vocal-like sound. In Example 3p the Db Major scale (Db Eb F Gb Ab Bb C) forms the basis of the lick and combines multiple legato and slide phrases to create its sound. Pick any string and challenge yourself to play the Minor Pentatonic scale and the Major scale using only that string.

Example 3p

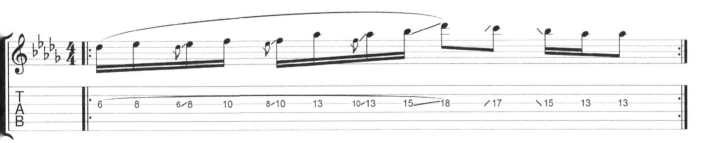

Applying bends to the one-string technique mentioned above can also create a melodic vocal-like line. Practis
to achieve precise bends and, once you feel comfortable, add some vibrato to them.

Example 3q

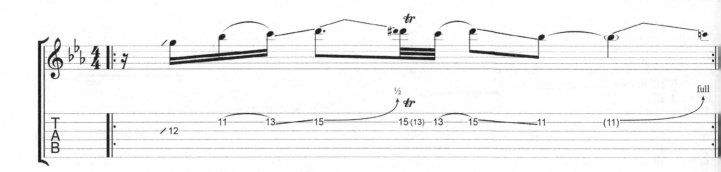

Chromatic ideas

The concept of adding chromatic passing tones to a scale is a huge one, so we will only touch on it briefly here
(For more information on how to use chromatics in your playing, check out Jens Larsen's *Modern Jazz Guita
Concepts* and Tim Pettingale's *Jazz Bebop Blues Guitar*).

Example 3r uses a repetitive pattern of chromatic notes (notes a semi-tone/one fret apart) and works well ove
both a B Major chord and an E Major chord.

Example 3r

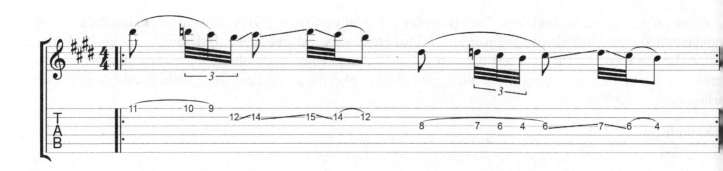

Playing standard scale shapes is all well and good, but in Neo-Soul, passing tones or chromatic notes are ofter
added to create extra tension and release. This idea is borrowed from jazz players and is commonly seen in the
style of players such as Pat Martino. Check out this YouTube video of Pat Martino and John Scofield, in which
they both use a ton of chromatic lines!

http://bit.ly/2OnoF3q

In Example 3s the E Major scale is combined with passing tones to create a slippery Neo-Soul lick that woul
work perfectly over any E Major chord, but frequently sits alongside an Emaj7 or Emaj9.

Refer to the neck diagram of the E Major scale in Example 3l if you need a reminder of this shape across the neck.

Example 3s

The next example sounds great over a IVmMaj7 to Imaj7 chord progression. In this case it's AmMaj7 to Emaj7. Slurred lines like these sound best when played freely and loosely as demonstrated in the audio example.

Example 3t

Having a certain level of dissonance is a common theme in Neo-Soul. This is usually achieved by using different types of altered dominant chords such as 7b5, 7#5, b9, #9 and b13. You will see voicings of these chords as you progress through this book, but keep in mind that their primary function is to add tension and they want to resolve, usually to a Major or Minor chord voicing.

In the next three examples we will show you some commonly used fills that can be applied to the chord at the end of each example. Once again, the concept of altered chords is a big one, so check out Joseph Alexander's book, *Chord Tone Soloing for Jazz Guitar* for more information.

Example 3u demonstrates the type of lick often played over altered chords in Neo-Soul. This line comes from the A Super Locrian scale (A B C C# Eb F G) – the seventh mode of the Melodic Minor scale.

Example 3u

Example 3v features the B Half-Whole Diminished scale (B C D D# E# F# G# A) and ends with a popular 13b9 voicing. The Half-Whole Diminished scale is frequently used to play over the 13b9 chord voicing shown in bar three and is a very popular scale choice among modern jazz, fusion and Neo-Soul guitarists.

Check out the popular Instagram guitarist Curt Henderson mixing modes of the Major scale with the Half-Whole Diminished scale in this video.

http://bit.ly/2QMyipf

Example 3v

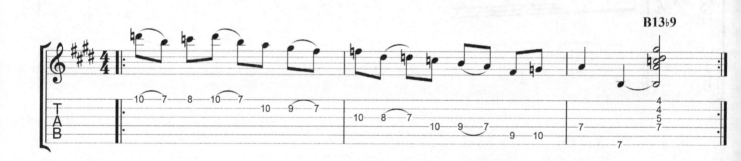

Example 3w uses a fluid legato line based around the E Super Locrian scale (E F G Ab Bb C D). This line was inspired by the great Robben Ford and his track *Talk To Your Daughter*. The great thing about Neo-Soul guitar parts is that they combine so many different genres into a "super genre"!

Example 3w

The final example in this chapter uses the B Major scale with an added G chromatic passing tone for extra tension, which resolves nicely to a Bmaj9 chord. The audio demonstrates this lick played both staccato (first time) and legato (second time). We recommend you practise it both ways.

Example 3x

Chapter Four – Double-Stop Lines

Artist Spotlight: Isaiah Sharkey

In terms of Neo-Soul, RnB and Gospel chops there are few better players to draw inspiration from than Isaiah Sharkey. Before making your way through this chapter, watch the YouTube video in the link below.

http://bit.ly/2PudPFx

A very recognisable sound in Neo-Soul guitar is the use of double-stops. Double-stops can be played in number of ways: with a pick, hybrid picking (pick and fingers) or only fingers. All of these approaches have a different sound, so experiment with these possibilities to see what works best for you. Incorporate the licks into your playing and transpose them to different keys, or just use them for inspiration to write your own.

To play the double-stop licks featured in this chapter with a pick, you have two main options:

Option number one is to use all down strokes. This is easier if you are new to this technique.

Option number two is to use alternate picking. It will take some practice to play the double-stops cleanly with alternate picking, but this approach will ultimately allow you to reach speeds you couldn't reach just using down strokes. As Isaiah Sharkey says with a smile on his face as he effortlessly alternate picks two strings a a time, "It's only two notes bro".

Exercises 4a to 4e use the A Minor Pentatonic scale (A C D E G) played simultaneously on two adjacent strings, and move through all five CAGED positions. If you are new to CAGED positions and would like more information on how they are formed and how to use them, check out Joseph Alexander's book *The CAGED System and 100 Licks for Blues Guitar*.

As you play these exercises, aim to keep both notes equal in both volume and duration. As always, start slowly increase the tempo, and aim to play as cleanly as possible.

Check out this amazing Instagram video to see this technique in action!

http://bit.ly/2CdEZNe

Example 4a

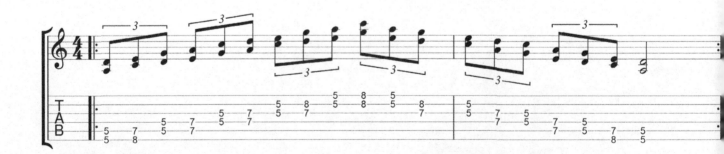

Example 4b

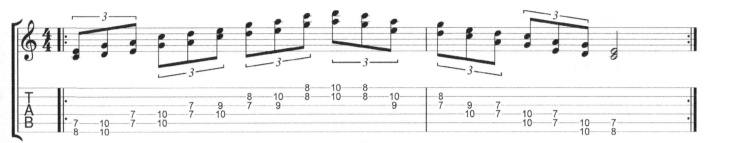

Example 4c

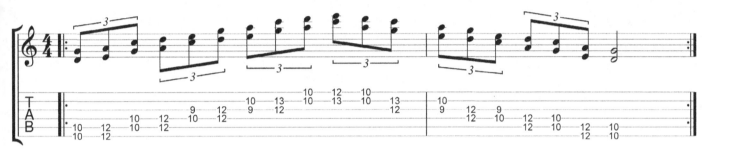

Example 4d

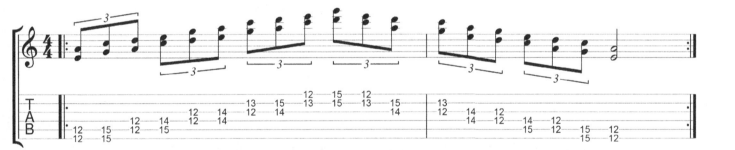

Example 4e

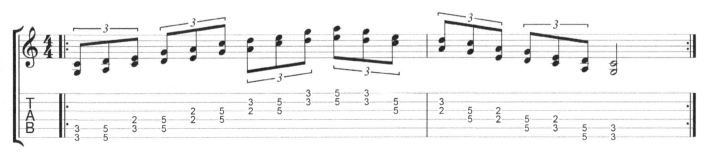

Now that you feel comfortable with the Pentatonic shapes, it's time to break out of the boxes. The next example moves up through the Pentatonic scale on two adjacent strings at a time.

The great thing about Neo-Soul is you can borrow from so many different genres. Check out Landon Jordan's playing on this super funky Prince track and pay attention his use of double-stop riffs.

http://bit.ly/2yjwAF3

Example 4f

Example 4g shows an A Minor Pentatonic scale double-stop pattern that skips between shapes to produce different intervals. It's amazing how many fresh ideas can be created using only the familiar box shapes. Commit these shapes to memory before moving on to the next examples.

Example 4g

Example 4h shows another double-stop exercise using the A Minor Pentatonic scale and string skipping. Remember to practise the licks demonstrated in this chapter along with the backing tracks provided with this book.

Example 4h

Now that you are familiar with the patterns, the following examples demonstrate musical licks and phrases using pentatonic double-stops. Example 4i once again uses the A Minor Pentatonic scale.

Example 4i

Example 4j demonstrates an A Minor Pentatonic scale double-stop phrase that uses multiple positions of the neck and has a memorable rhythmic pattern. Make sure you listen to the audio of this example before you play it yourself, so you can hear the subtleties in the phrasing.

Example 4j

Example 4k is based around the C# Minor Pentatonic scale (C# E F# G# B) and has a funky syncopated groove. Make sure you complete the final sliding lick with your first finger only.

This idea was the basis for Kristof's Instagram video below.

http://bit.ly/2EiMIMu

Example 4k

Until now, the exercises in this chapter have focused on the Pentatonic scale. The next few examples use all seven notes of the Major scale. Example 4l uses 3rds from the C Major scale (C D E F G A B). Record a little loop of a Cmaj7 chord and practise this lick as demonstrated below, then jam your own ideas as well. Remember that a quick way to get double the mileage out of all of these licks is to reverse them and play them from the end to the beginning too!

If the concept of intervals is new to you and you would like to learn more, check out Joseph Alexander's book *The Practical Guide To Modern Music Theory For Guitarists*.

Example 4l

Example 4m demonstrates playing the E Major scale (E F# G# A B C# D#) in 3rd intervals using only the D and G strings. Using the interval of a 3rd is a great way to outline chords and this lick would work brilliantly over an Emaj7 or an Emaj9 chord.

Example 4m

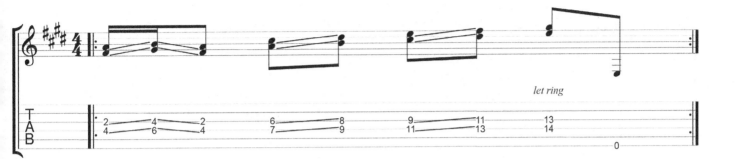

A popular double-stop device in Neo-Soul is to use an interval of a 4th. In this example, the C Major scale (C D E F G A B) is the basis for a commonly used double-stop lick. Play this lick as smoothly as possible.

Example 4n

Example 4o is built around the A Major scale (A B C# D E F# G#). This lick introduces the "palm mute" (resting your hand gently near the bridge to deaden the strings slightly, so they don't ring out) and shows how it can be used with double-stops to evoke the Neo-Soul sound. We recommend you practise this technique by palm-muting all the early examples in this book.

Example 4o

The next examples uses double-stops in 5ths. Example 4p shows a sliding pattern on the D and G strings using the E Major scale. The double-stop element of this lick works well over an Emaj7 or Emaj9 chord.

Example 4p

It is important when learning any new techniques on the guitar to play it in multiple ways. In the previous example we demonstrated the use of 5ths on two adjacent strings. Example 4q uses 5ths from E Major on different string sets. This may be more challenging to play at first, but is well worth the effort as this sound really captures the Neo-Soul flavour.

Example 4q

Another popular interval choice for double-stop licks in Neo-Soul is the 6th. Example 4r is a rhythmic idea that uses triplets, 1/16th notes and 1/8th notes and is based around the G Major scale (G A B C D E F#). The sound of the 6th interval will likely be quite familiar to you, as it is extremely popular in blues, country, folk and pop as well as Neo-Soul.

Example 4r

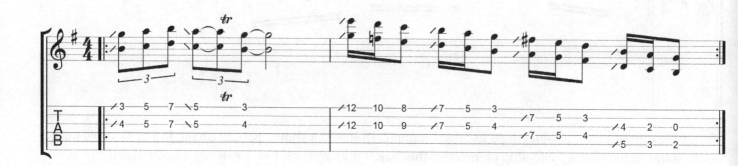

Example 4s demonstrates a double-stop lick created using the interval of a 6th and is based around the E Major scale. The second bar has a chromatic movement that is popular in blues as well as Neo-Soul.

Example 4s

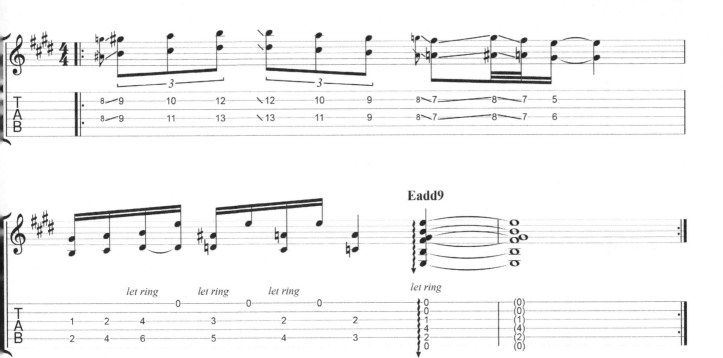

Although the examples above illustrate the most commonly used intervals when playing double-stop licks, the examples below are well worth investigating to explore some fresh new sounds. Example 4t is based around the A Major Scale and centres around the interval of a 2nd.

Example 4t

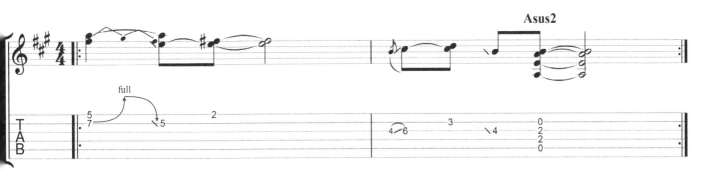

The interval of a 7th is somewhat dissonant, but can be a fun extra element to add into your Neo-Soul lick bag. Example 4u demonstrates how to use the interval of a 7th with a Neo-Soul flavour based around the E Major scale. Try this lick out over an Emaj7 or an Emaj9 chord.

Example 4u

Now let's put all these interval ideas together. This is where things get really interesting. Example 4v uses mixture of 3rds and 4ths using the D Natural Minor scale (D E F G A Bb C). This idea would work well ove a Dm7 or a Dm9 chord.

Example 4v

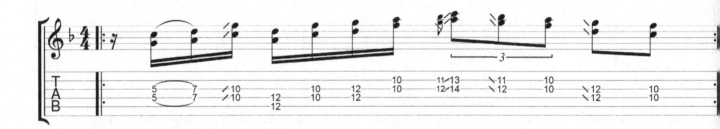

Example 4w shows a lick we both love to play. It is based around the C Major scale and starts off with combination of 4ths and 3rds in bar one. Bar two is a Cmaj7 chord, but between each note of the chord a not from the C Major scale is added. This is a technique we both learnt from Beau Diakowicz. Make sure th Cmaj7 chord in the last bar rings out.

Example 4w

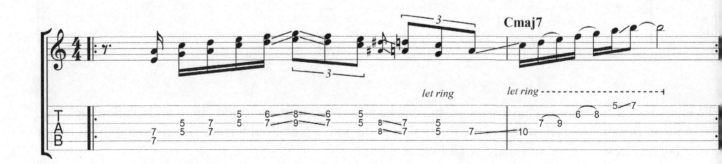

The last three examples of this chapter go beyond double-stops by incorporating them into chord sequences and phrases. Example 4x is based around the D Major scale (D E F# G A B C#) and combines chord shapes, a single note line, and a multiple double-stops to create a beautiful two-bar D Major phrase.

Example 4x

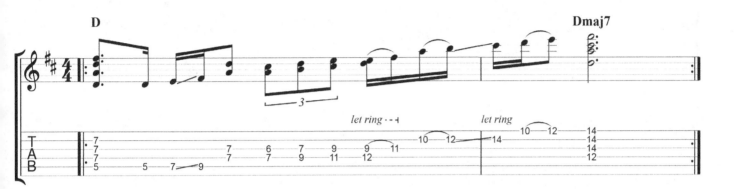

A lot of the content in this book may feel somewhat removed from more traditional blues and rock licks, but Example 4y shows how you can bring some Hendrix-esque vibe to your Neo-Soul playing. Based around the E Major Pentatonic scale (E F# G# B C#), the patterns in this lick are reminiscent of tracks such as *The Wind Cries Mary*.

Example 4y

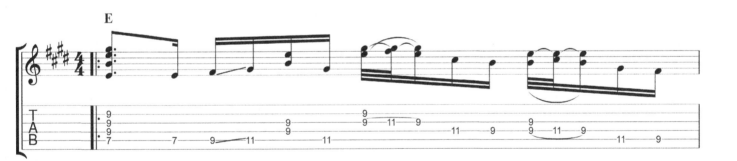

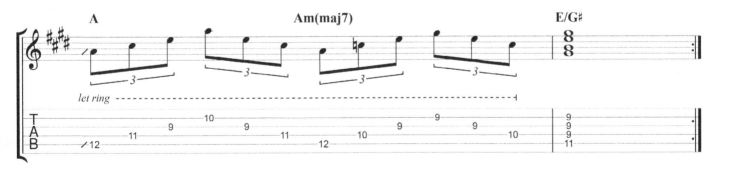

Example 4z uses the C Major scale and is once again rooted in early Hendrix-style double-stops. It has been modernised with position shifts to give it a more Neo-Soul sound. The main aim with this lick is to let all the notes ring out as much as possible.

Example 4z

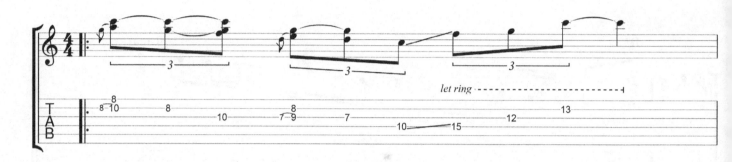

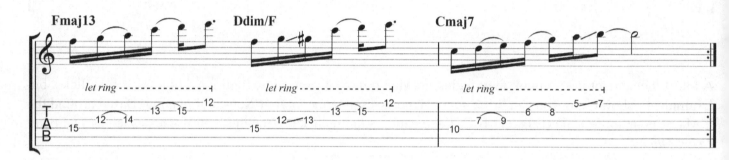

Check out Curt Henderson and Alexander Coombs, who use a variety of techniques including double-stops. Have a look at Curt's video on Instagram in the link below.

http://bit.ly/2Pvbr1g

Chapter Five – Grooves

Artist Spotlight: Curt Henderson, Todd Pritchard, Kerry "2 Smooth" Marshall, Mark Lettieri

In this chapter we aim to provide you with a wealth of chord voicings and melodic fills. More importantly, we will show you how to blend them together into Neo-Soul groove patterns. As you learn the examples featured throughout this chapter, experiment and create your own grooves based on each one. Remember, when it comes to music you cannot steal enough!

The inspiration for the grooves in this chapter came from a wide variety of players including Curt Henderson, Todd Pritchard, Kerry "2 Smooth" Marshall, Mark Lettieri and many others. Before you start playing through these grooves, check out these four short Instagram videos packed with so much groove it will be tough to stop your foot tapping and head nodding!

http://bit.ly/2yynh3n

http://bit.ly/2QKIHSh

http://bit.ly/2CEksCh

http://bit.ly/2RIAEGZ

Example 5a demonstrates a Major 9 chord groove. A common feature of Neo-Soul is to disregard conventional chord theory and move a shape that sounds fantastic through multiple keys. This example demonstrates the concept by moving a Major 9 chord shape through the keys of A, E, G and D.

For bonus points, play this example using fingerpicking, picking, and hybrid-picking (pick and fingers). The same groove can sound quite different when played in these three different ways.

Example 5a

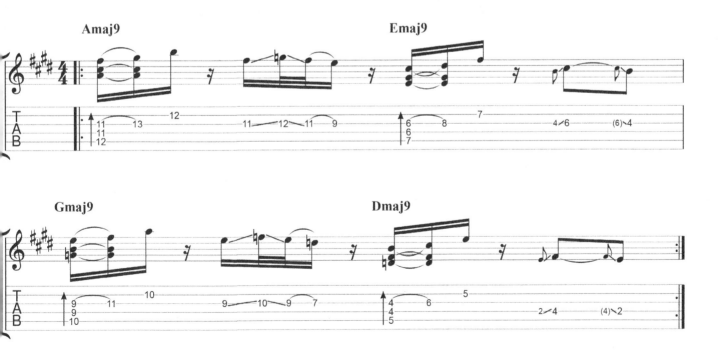

A super cool trick used in Neo-Soul guitar parts is the "chord quake" or "slip and slide". In Example 5b, pla
a Major 9 chord shape and slide from each chord tone to one fret below and back again. You can apply thi
technique to any chord shape, not just the Major 9 chords shown in this example.

Example 5b

We've seen that a common trick used in Neo-Soul is to palm-mute chord shapes. Gently rest your picking han
across the strings near the bridge and don't push too hard on the strings. A soft palm mute works really we
for this style of chordal work.

In the groove below there is a "call and response" pattern: two bars are palm muted and two bars are playe
with the chords allowed to ring out.

Example 5c

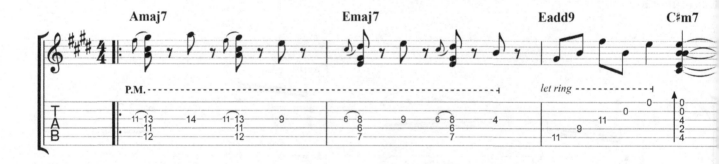

54

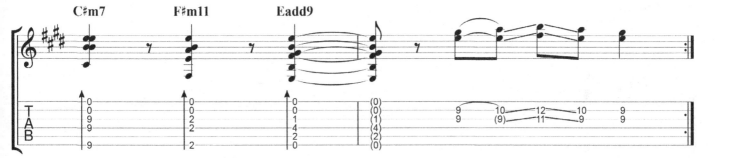

One of our favourite sounds in Neo-Soul is the IVm cadence. Although the trick of converting the IV chord of a key from major to minor goes back beyond The Beatles, it is still prominent today. In this example the chord progression alternates between Dmaj7 and Gmaj7, and adds the Gm9 chord (IVm) to create a stronger pull back to the home chord of Dmaj7.

Example 5d

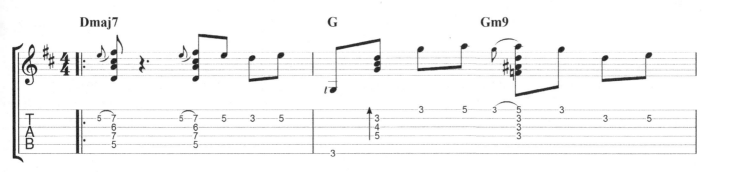

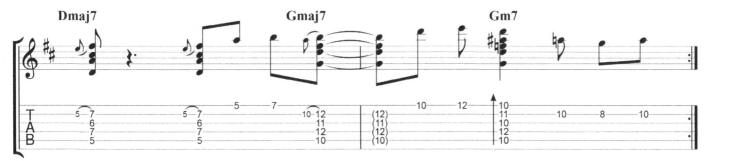

Example 5e illustrates commonly used Maj9 and Maj7 voicings in E and A, and introduces a popular altered dominant chord in Neo-Soul in the form of G#7#5#9. The addition of double-stops at the end of bar two make this E Major groove distinctly Neo-Soul.

Example 5e

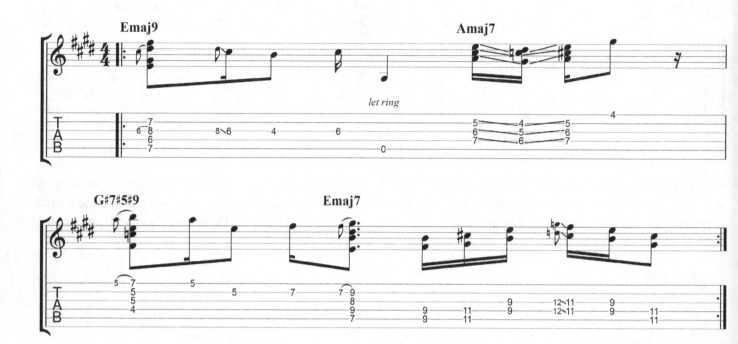

Incorporating open strings into licks is another device used frequently in Neo-Soul. E Major is a great place to write licks on the guitar that include open strings, since they really suit this key, as demonstrated in Example 5f. Aim to let the open B and high E strings ring out as you move the chords in the first three bars of this example. The A/B to B13b9 movement in bar four is a really cool Neo-Soul chord progression. Take note of this one!

Example 5f

Now add this slippery E Major scale (E F# G# A B C# D#) legato fill to the chords in the previous example.

Example 5g

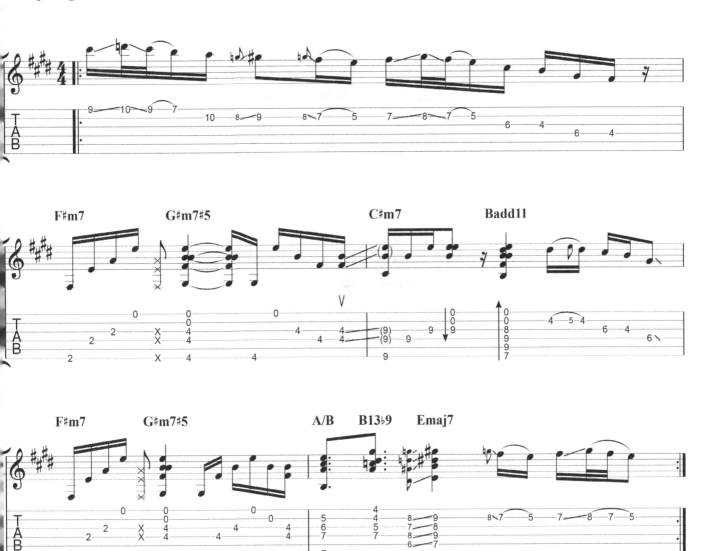

Example 5h is reminiscent of the first Neo-Soul guitar part Simon ever heard. He was instantly hooked on the complex, modern sounding chord shapes and melodic fills, and we're sure you will be too!

This example is in the key of E Minor and uses partial chord fragments that are predominantly based around the top four strings. This is a common strategy in Neo-Soul and jazz as it leaves space for a bassline.

Example 5h

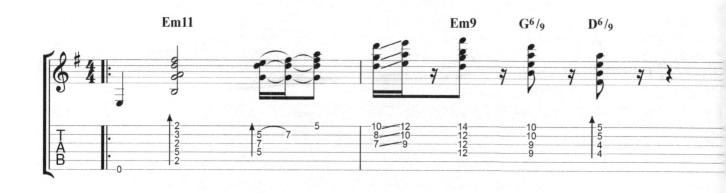

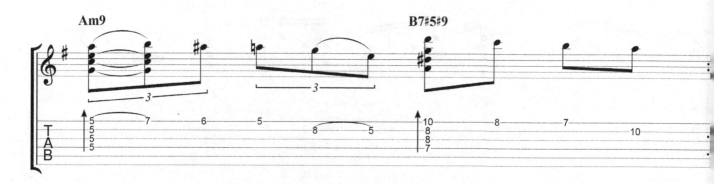

Here is a Gospel-style chord progression that includes slash chords and ends with a smooth D Major scale (D E F# G A B C#) run. If you would like more information on slash chords check out Simon's lesson in the link below.

https://www.fundamental-changes.com/Major-slash-chords-video-guitar-lesson/

Example 5i

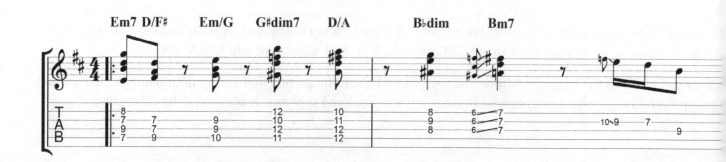

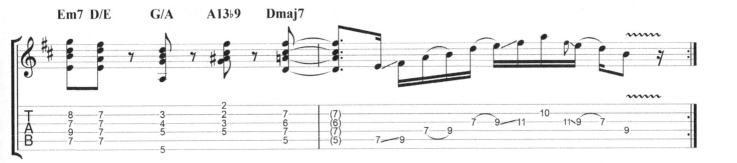

Quartal voicings (chords built entirely from 4ths) are very popular in Neo-Soul. The G#m11 chord at the start of bar one and the E6/9 shape at the start of bar two are the most common quartal chord shapes used in this genre. This gives you a voicing to use from the A string root and the D string root.

Example 5j

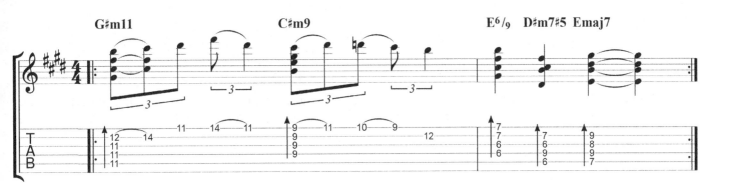

Example 5k demonstrates some gorgeous chord voicings based predominantly around a Dmaj7 vamp. The addition of the diminished chords in bar six is another popular chordal trick used in Neo-Soul, as they add a sense of dissonance, but also act as passing chords between the Dmaj7 and the Bm7.

Example 5k

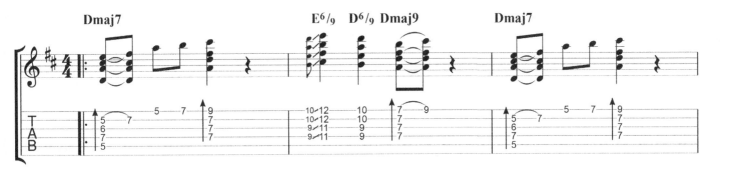

Example 51 includes one of our favourite chord tricks in this whole book. The slide using the Cmaj9 chord in bar one is a technique we include frequently in our compositions. Make sure you steal this one! This chord sequence is in the key of C Major and has an RnB vibe reminiscent of Kerry "2 Smooth" Marshall, Spanky Alford and Isaiah Sharkey.

Example 5l

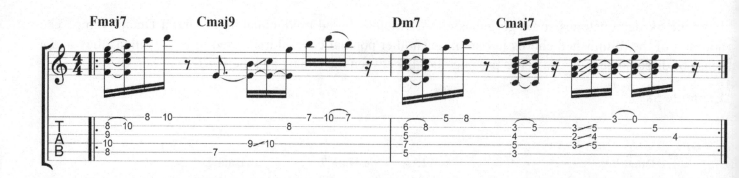

Simon first heard these Gospel style chord voicings with a high E pedal note played by incredible acoustic guitarist Tommy Emmanuel. In Example 5m, try to let the high E note ring out as clearly as possible as you change through each shape.

Example 5m

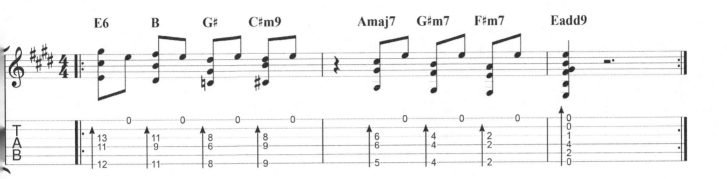

This example is in the key of B Minor and packs many of the techniques shown in this book into four bars, including common Neo-Soul chord voicings, legato techniques and double-stops. The more grooves like this you learn by heart the better. Pick your favourites and spend extra time committing them to memory.

Practise each chord change in Example 5n individually and build this example up slowly, especially if these chord shapes are new to you.

Example 5n

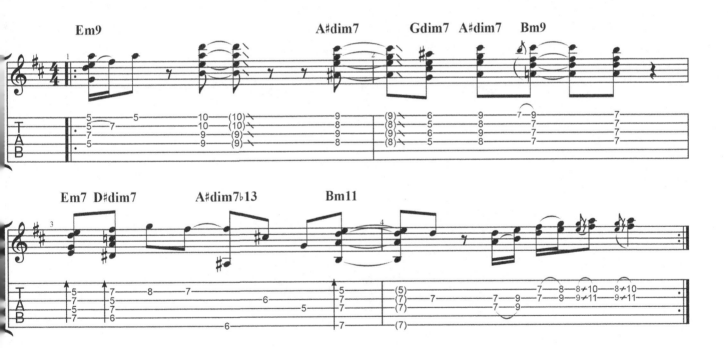

When practising Example 5o, play the legato lines separately to the chords before joining them together. Aim to achieve a "flowing" sound when playing this example. Imagine creating the sound of a cascading waterfall when completing the E Major scale (E F# G# A B C# D#) hammer-ons and pull-offs.

Example 5o

The groove in Example 5p was taken from an Instagram video Simon performed.

http://bit.ly/2yewpLi

This longer groove is in the key of G Minor and centres around the three-chord progression of Ebmaj9, Bbmaj9 and Gm11. The G Minor Pentatonic scale (G Bb C D F) provides the main notes for the single-notes and double-stop licks you see throughout, but there are some occasional passing notes for extra colour.

Example 5p

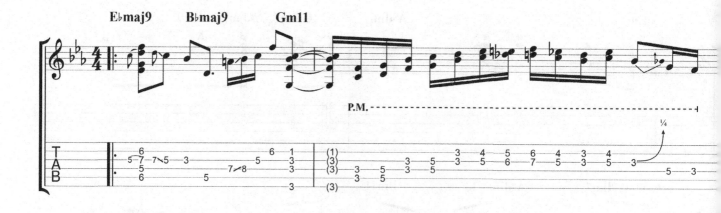

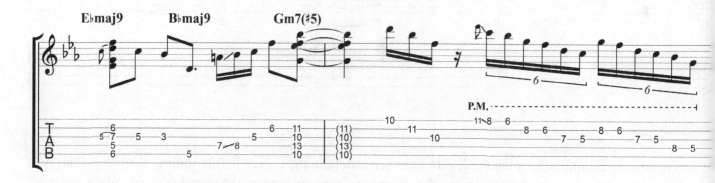

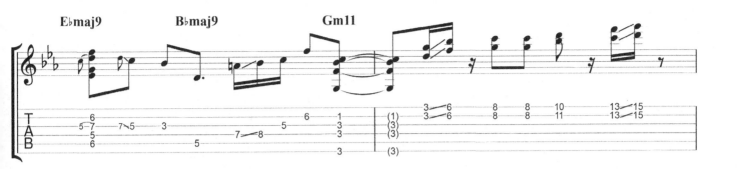

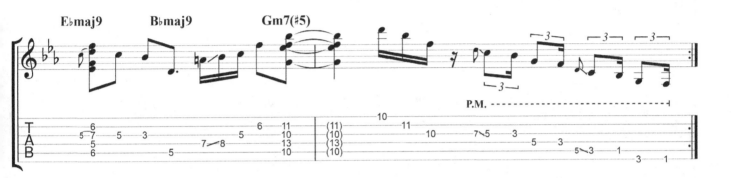

Often a Neo-Soul chordal part will include a melodic phrase which is generally played on the B and high E strings. Check out how this is achieved in the key of Eb Major in Example 5q.

With this example you may find it easier to learn the chord shapes first, then the melody lines on the B and E strings separately. Only add them together when you are comfortable with both parts.

Example 5q

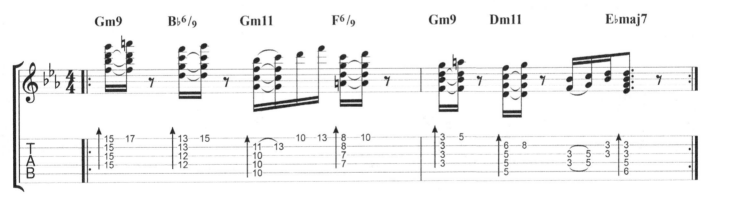

There are some beautiful voicings included in Example 5r. The Major 7 voicings in bars two and three, and the 13b9 voicing at the end of bar five are well worth adding to your chord arsenal.

Example 5r

This example is one of our favourite grooves in this chapter. It is based around the key of B Minor and for most of the groove uses the B Minor Pentatonic scale (B D E F# A). In bar two, the groove briefly moves into A Minor, where the A Blues scale (A C D Eb E G) is used for a popular descending Neo-Soul Pattern. The lick ends in bar four with an F# Altered scale (F# G A Bb C D E) run. This lick is ultra-hip and modern sounding and will definitely impress your friends!

We recommend that you play this example using hybrid-picking (pick and fingers).

Example 5s

When we were studying and preparing the content for this book, we spent time digging deep into jazz chord voicings as well as traditional Neo-Soul artists. This idea came from Barry Galbraith, who is arguably one of the greatest jazz guitarists who ever lived, yet quite unknown by the majority of guitarists. We highly recommend you check out his book, *Guitar Comping*, but bear in mind that it is notation only and has no tab.

Example 5t is in the key of E Major and uses a complex set of altered dominant chords which provide a lot of tension in the first two bars, before resolving to the Emaj9 in bar three. Make sure you fully fret the barre chord shape seen in bar four and hold it down as you complete the legato patterns.

Example 5t

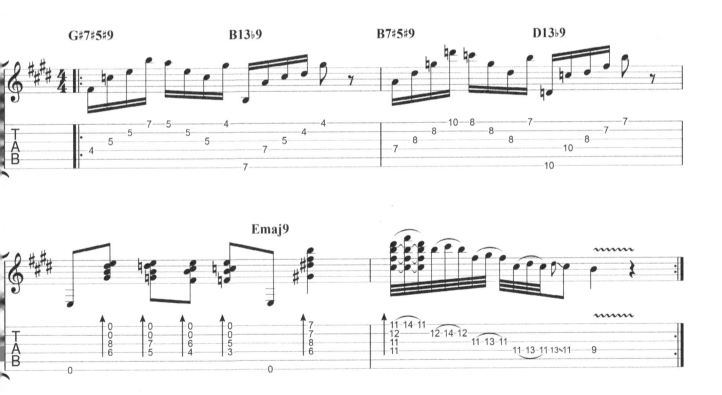

Sometimes, the chord shapes used in Neo-Soul sound great using an arpeggio pattern, as demonstrated in Example 5u, but don't work so well when played with a strumming pattern. When you are writing your own Neo-Soul grooves, experiment with both arpeggios and strumming (or a combination of both) and see which sounds best. This groove is in the key of G# Minor.

Example 5u

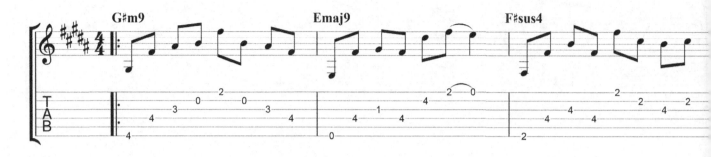

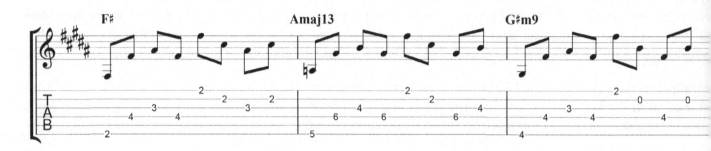

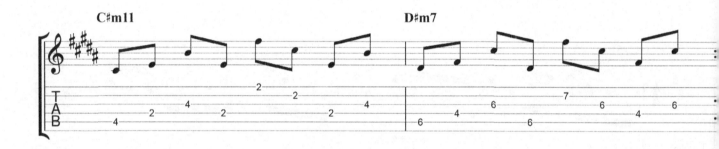

Example 5v is in the key of D Minor and illustrates the technique of palm muting barre chords. In other genre such as rock it is quite common to palm mute single notes, but Neo-Soul takes that a stage further and applie it to multi-string chords. Experiment with this example first, but then go back over the grooves featured in thi chapter and see if adding in palm mutes brings a different flavour to them.

Example 5v

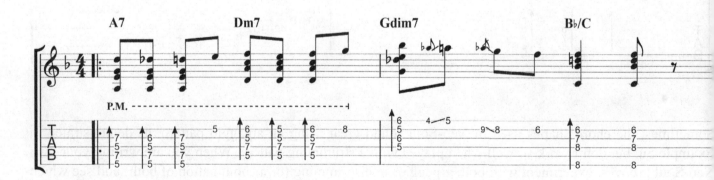

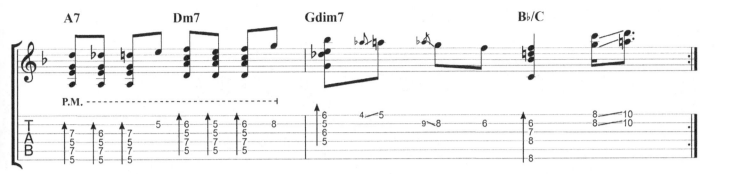

By now it should be apparent that the combination of chords and fills is a large part of the Neo-Soul sound. One thing to bear in mind is that the fills you use between the chords should never detract from the underlying groove. To build your discipline in this area, make sure you work with a metronome to play all the examples in this book, and pay close attention to getting the changes tight and "in the pocket".

Example 5w is in the key of E Major and was inspired by watching several Todd Pritchard videos. As well as using the examples featured in this book we recommend following the artists we have mentioned on Instagram and absorbing as many ideas as you can from them.

Example 5w

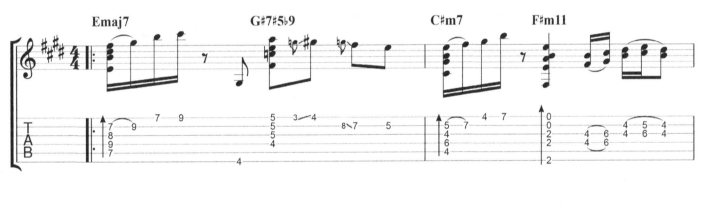

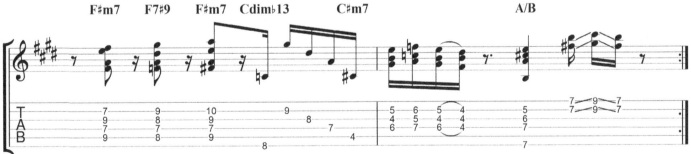

Quartet guitar playing (a sub-genre of Gospel music) is so closely linked to Neo-Soul that we wanted to include a longer groove in this style. This piece is in the key of E and uses slash chords with a descending bassline pattern. Watch Simon play it on the video link below.

https://www.fundamental-changes.com/neo-soul-videos/

Example 5x – Better In Fours

Chapter Six – Extended Techniques

Artist Spotlight: Justus West

So far we've covered many of the different techniques that contribute to the Neo-Soul sound, but this chapter will take your playing to a whole new level! The extended techniques in this chapter include a more in-depth look at the "chord quake", hammer-ons from nowhere, chromatic approach notes, tapping, natural harmonics, artificial harmonics and much more. Don't worry, each technique is demonstrated in a video, as well as notated below. Make sure you watch each video as you progress through the techniques. (**https://www.fundamental changes.com/neo-soul-videos/**)

Before you dive in, watch this Justus West Instagram video below. We guarantee you will be blown away by some of the playing featured here.

http://bit.ly/2QNdj5x

Example 6a shows the famous chord quake first mentioned in Chapter Five. The speedy slides are to be executed while holding down the chord shapes written above the music. Play the first chord tone, then slide down one fret and back up to the chord tone. Play the next chord tone, allowing the first string you played to continue to ring, and so on. You should hear a gentle cascading effect. Make sure to play this as cleanly as possible before you speed up. If this technique is new to you, we recommend you spend some time practising each bar individually before combining them into this four-bar example.

Example 6a

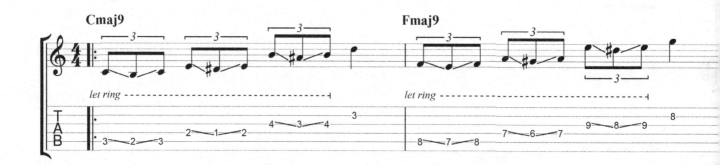

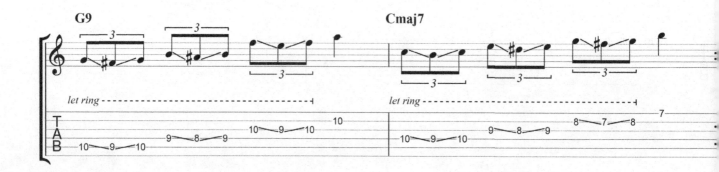

Until now, we have demonstrated the chord quake technique by picking the individual notes of a larger chord voicing. Example 6b demonstrates how to apply it using double stops around the E Major Scale (E F# G# A B C# D#). This example will work particularly well over an Emaj7 or Emaj9 chord.

Example 6b

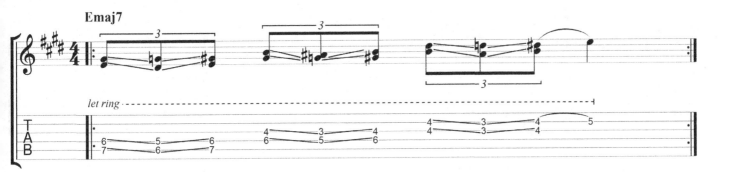

Now let's put the chord quake into a more musical context by adding it into a longer line based around the C Major scale (C D E F G A B). Make sure you hold down the Cmaj7 shape in bar two when completing the chord quake.

Example 6c

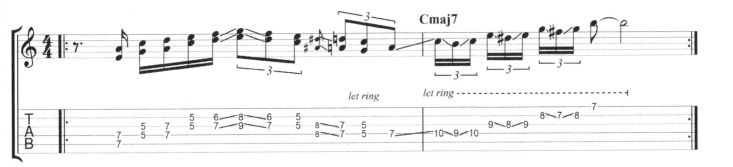

Example 6d demonstrates a slide-style vibrato that was made famous by the rock fusion master Greg Howe. He isn't known for playing Neo-Soul, but is heavily associated with this type of vibrato and the technique is often used by Neo-Soul guitar players. The goal is to slide the fingers of the fretting hand outside of the fret (usually up) then return to pitch. Don't move the fingers around within a fret to create the vibrato, instead slide up, out of the fret, and back down to pitch. Do this quickly, multiple times, to create a heavier vibrato. To see this technique in action, watch the video below.

Example 6d illustrates this technique with a lick built around the A Blues scale (A C D Eb E G). This lick will work well over an Am7 or Am9 chord.

https://www.fundamental-changes.com/neo-soul-videos/

Example 6d

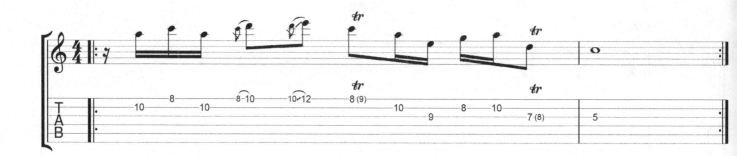

We can take the Greg Howe vibrato idea one step further and use it with double-stops. Example 6e is a G# Minor Pentatonic scale (G# B C# D# F#) phrase built entirely out of double-stops. It uses hammer-ons, slides and the Greg Howe vibrato to give it the Neo-Soul sound. This lick works well over a Gm7 or Gm9 chord.

Listen to the audio of the next example, but feel free to experiment with the length and width of your own vibrato. It sounds different when you slide between the 4th and 5th fret once (subtle vibrato), compared to sliding between the 4th and 6th fret multiple times (heavy vibrato). You can slide even further, if that's the sound you prefer!

Example 6e

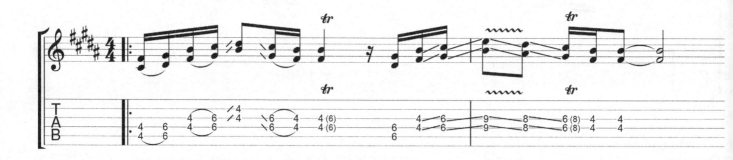

Example 6f is a fun chord progression in D Major that incorporates the use of an augmented chord in bar one. This adds to the tension before resolving to the Bm9 chord in bar two. In this example, the chord quake technique is applied to the full chord shape of a C#dim7 (at the end of bar two).

Example 6f

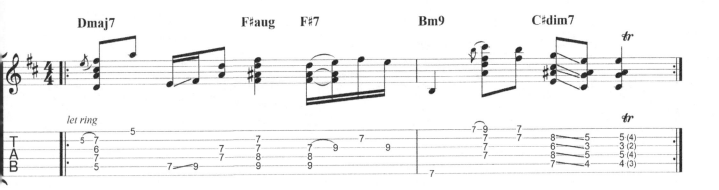

The next technique we'll look at is a more advanced take on Chapter Two's RnB chord tricks. It is a common Neo-Soul approach to run down a chord shape. Example 6g demonstrates this approach around a Cmaj7 chord voicing. Aim to pick each note clearly and use alternate picking to play this exercise.

Example 6g

Example 6h is predominantly based around the C Major Pentatonic scale (C D E G A) and introduces the popular legato technique of hammer-ons from nowhere.

Hammer-ons and pull-offs will help you achieve greater speed, especially "hammer-ons from nowhere" which will make your licks sound very fluent. The fretting hand does almost all of the work in this example. When changing strings, hammer your finger down without picking and aim to make all the notes the same volume. End the lick with a chord quake using the Cmaj9 chord. Play this lick freely, because fluency is key here.

Example 6h

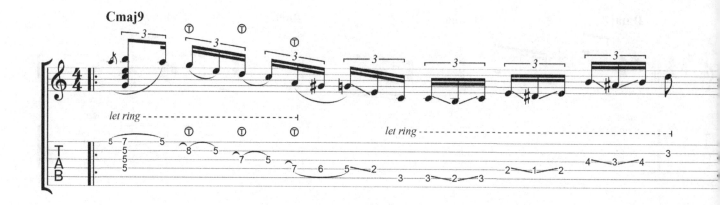

Example 6i demonstrates a chord progression in the key of D Major that relies heavily on the use of fretting hand legato patterns to create its fluid sound. Although it may look daunting at first, bar two will feel familiar as you have already learnt the pattern in Example 6g, though now it is played in D Major instead of C Major.

Example 6i

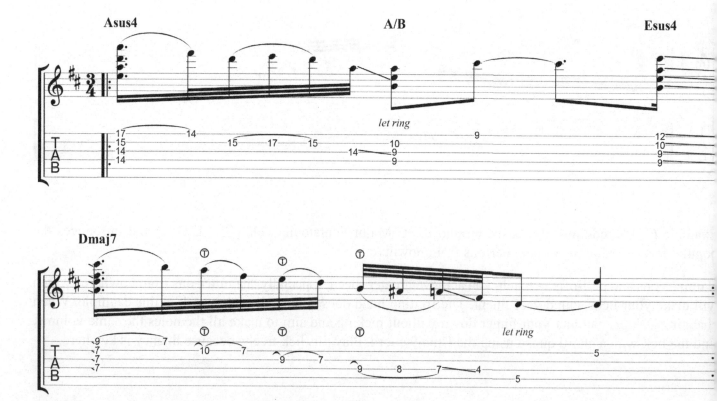

Example 6j shows a cool legato line based around the C Major Scale. The first half of bar one demonstrates a legato sequence based on an Em11 chord. The second half of the bar ascends with a mixture of an Fmaj arpeggio (F A C E) and Cmaj7 arpeggio (C E G B) before resolving to the Cmaj7 voicing on the top four strings.

Example 6j

The following two examples use chromatic approach notes with double-stop lines. Start a semitone below the chord tones, slide into them and re-pick the notes. Palm mute these passages to control the volume of the approach notes and let the last notes ring out to reinforce the key. If you are new to playing this style of double-stop, we recommend using all downstrokes.

Example 6k

Example 6l shows a palm muted double-stop pattern on multiple strings. Although the end of the bar resolves beautifully to D Major, the rest of the bar also fits well over an E Major or E7 chord.

Example 6l

Although tapping is a technique not closely associated with Neo-Soul, it can create some very interesting sounds and enables us to include notes in our lines that would otherwise be out of reach. Example 6m holds down an E Major barre chord using the CAGED E shape at the 12th fret, while executing a tap across all strings on the 16th fret. All of the sound is created by the picking hand, while the fretting hand holds the chord. Below is a link to a video giving a detailed description of this tapping technique.

https://www.fundamental-changes.com/neo-soul-videos/

Example 6m

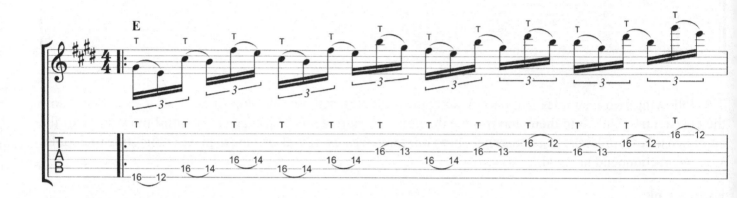

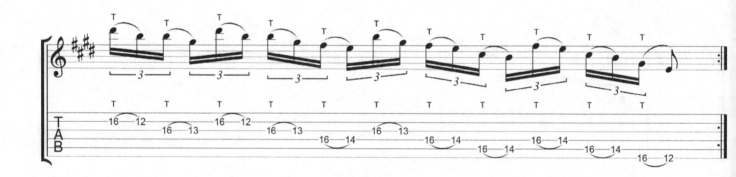

The next lick uses more than one finger of the picking hand. For most people it will be easiest to use the middle and ring fingers, especially if you are holding a pick, but test out other finger combinations (index and middle, index and ring, middle and pinky) to see what works best for you. The idea of the lick remains the same. Hold down an E Major barre chord on the 12th fret while tapping with the picking hand, but now tap two strings simultaneously.

Example 6n

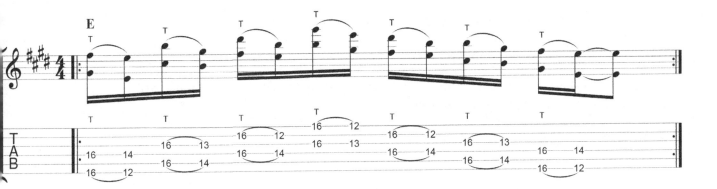

When the use of both hands on the fretboard is comfortable for you, move on to Example 6o to apply this technique in a more musical context. This example has a slightly swung groove and is in the key of E Major, so each mini-lick can be played over an Emaj7 or an Emaj9 chord. Note the use of the 6/4 time signature too. Listen to how Kristof plays this example on the audio track to get the feel of the 6/4 time before you play it.

Example 6o

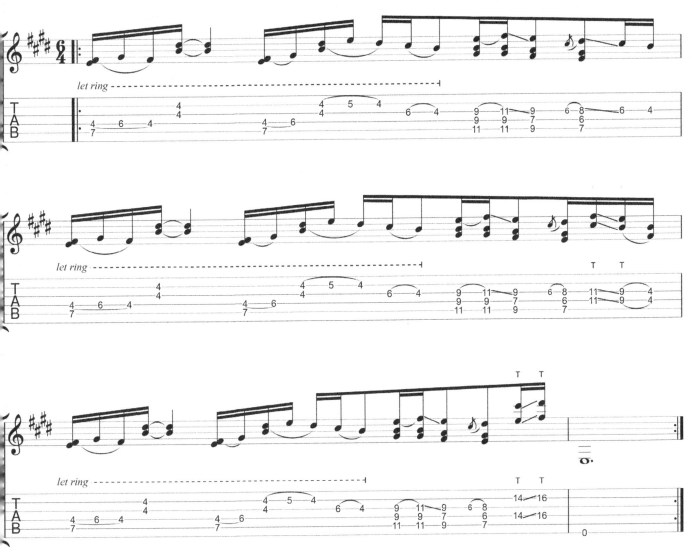

Natural harmonics are available all over the fretboard. Example 6p illustrates some ideas of how to use them with a chord progression in the key of G Major.

For more information on natural harmonics check out Rob Thorpe's fantastic article on harmonics below.

https://www.fundamental-changes.com/natural-harmonics-part-2/

The last beat of bar three is a "behind the nut bend". To complete this bend, push down on the string behind the nut to raise the harmonic by a semitone.

Example 6p

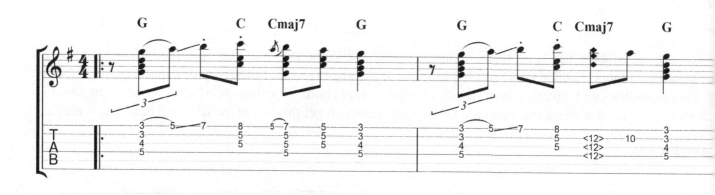

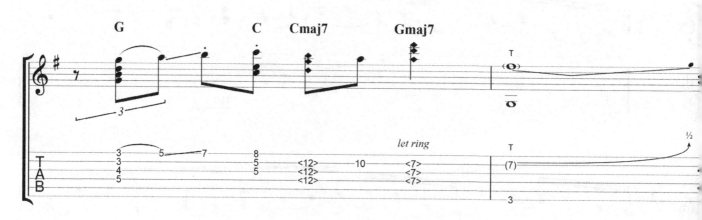

Natural harmonics are beautiful, but their use can be a little limited. The answer to this limitation is provided by artificial harmonics. Make sure you watch the video for a detailed explanation of how to create artificial harmonics, as there is more than one way to do so.

The easiest way for pick users to execute artificial harmonics is to hold the pick between the thumb and middle finger. Fingerpickers should use the nail of the thumb of the picking hand.

Point to twelve frets above the fretted note with the index finger of the picking hand and lightly touch the string while you pluck it with the pick or thumb. For example, fret the 7th fret on the G string and lightly touch the 19th fret of the same string with the index finger of the picking hand, as you point to the metal of the fret. Now pick or pluck behind the index finger. The result should be a sound similar to a natural harmonic.

Work on picking the artificial harmonic cleanly before continuing with Example 6q. This example introduces these sweet sounding harmonics with a progression using the E Major scale. Pay extra attention to the last bar as the harmonics are played seven frets above the fretted notes this time, to create a different interval.

Example 6q

Example 6r demonstrates a different execution of artificial harmonics. The "slap tap" means that you have to slap or hit the fret twelve frets above the fretted note (or notes in this example). This is also explained in detail in the included video.

This example is in the key of E Major and Kristof recorded it at 70 beats per minute. You can experiment with different tempos with all the licks in this book as you become comfortable playing them.

Example 6r

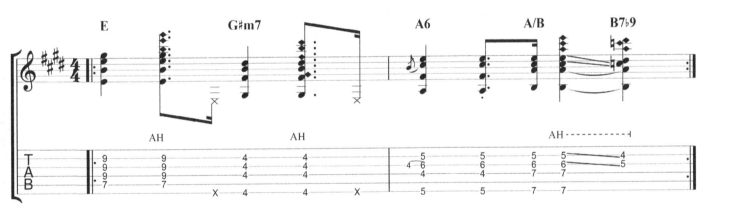

The next five examples combine the above techniques with some interesting chord voicings. Example 6s is in the key of G Major and uses the G Major Pentatonic scale (G A B D E) with some chromaticism to create a modern sounding Neo-Soul phrase. We recommend practising the chord shapes shown in this example on their own before playing through the full example.

Example 6s

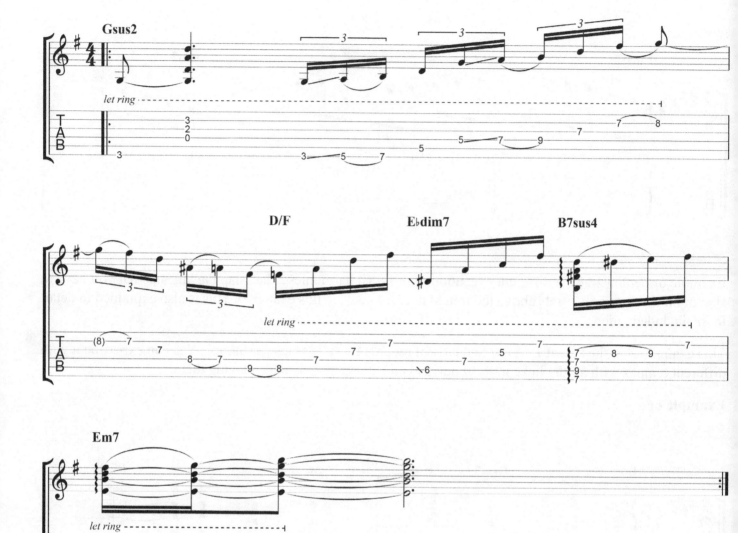

Example 6t is a mixture of tapping and chord voicings that revolve around the key of D Major. Use two fingers of the fretting hand to tap frets seventeen and nineteen on the high E string. You can also slide from the seventeenth to nineteenth fret and back if you prefer that sound. The fluidity that these extended techniques can create is a large part of the complex Neo-Soul sound. To see this technique in action check out the video below.

http://bit.ly/2Om5K9l

Example 6t

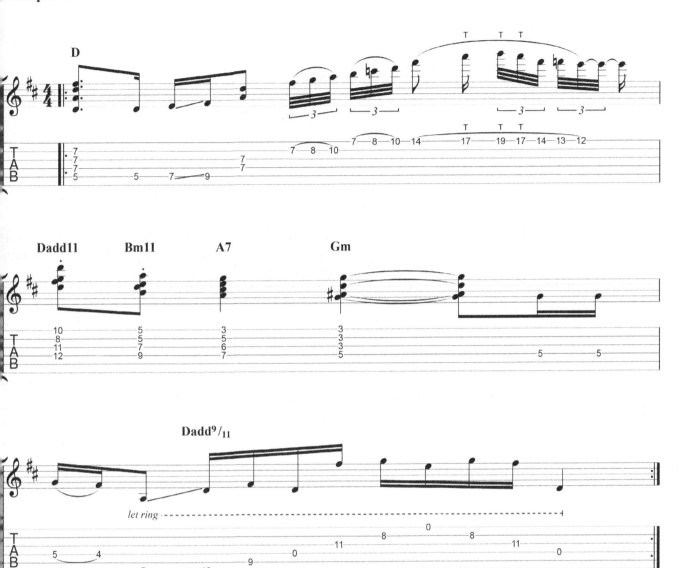

There are two main ways to play fast on the guitar: playing in a rigid, rhythmic pattern as fast as you can, or cramming as many notes as possible into a bar and making sure you land on a specific beat. Example 6u demonstrates the second way of playing fast by cramming a lot of notes into a beat and a half. Make sure you land on beat three when completing this example.

This example uses the C Major Scale (C D E F G A B) and works well over a CMaj7 or a CMaj9 chord.

Example 6u

Example 6v combines legato, hammer-ons from nowhere, triple-stops and harmonics in the key of C Major (C D E F G A B C). As with a lot of Neo-Soul licks and phrases, bar three is meant to be played loosely, so don worry about being completely on top of the click when performing this example.

Example 6v

The last example of this chapter is the most advanced. It seeks to combine many of the different technique we've explored without sacrificing musicality. This lick is based around F Major and uses the F Major scale (G A Bb C D E) in bars one and two, with some added chromatic passing notes. Bar three combines a Bbmaj (Bb D F A) and Bbm (Bb Db F) arpeggio to create the IVmaj to IVm cadence. The example ends with gorgeous ascending F Major double-stop pattern.

Make sure you listen to the audio example, as the second time it is played in free time. Experiment with thi and make each note sound as clean as possible.

Example 6w

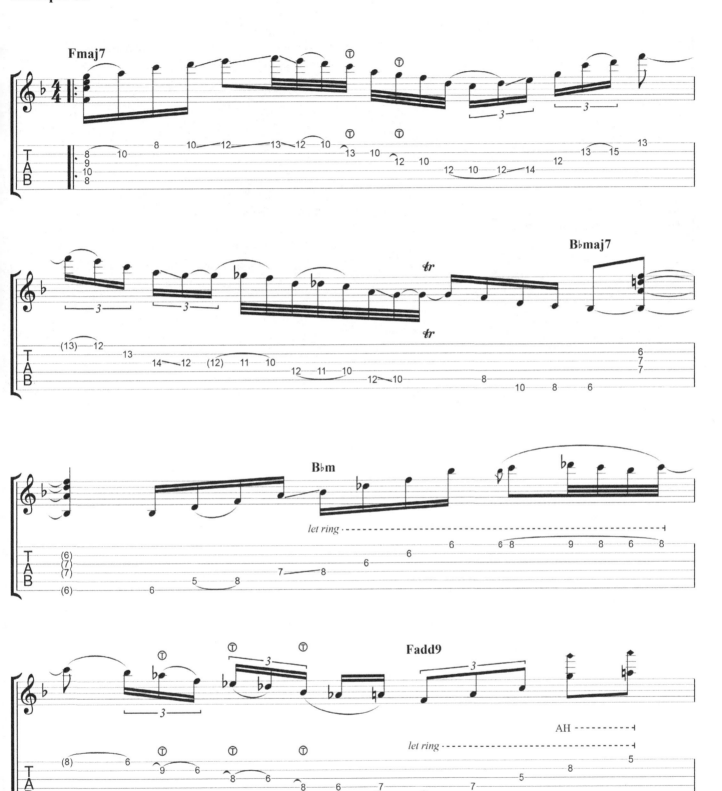

Chapter Seven – Mark Lettieri's "Coastin'"

It's an honour to be able to include a chapter about one of our personal guitar heroes. Mark Lettieri is one of the most innovative, musical, and technical players around and included in this book are two original pieces written by Mark for you to learn.

Coastin' is in the key of D Major (D E F# G A B C#) and has a relaxed funk groove. It consists of jazz chord voicings, legato fills, and signature Lettieri techniques such as the use of the whammy bar. Read the following tips before tackling this piece and be sure to watch the full video below.

https://www.fundamental-changes.com/neo-soul-videos/

The track starts out with Major 7 and Minor 7 chords with a syncopated groove in the key of D.

Mark uses the whammy bar a lot at the beginning of *Coastin'*. For example in bar three, play the Bm7add9 chord and slide the shape up a tone to play C#m7add9. When you have completed the slide, press the whammy bar down a full tone before releasing it to return to pitch. Mark uses this idea often and it's a fun technique to add to your Neo-Soul playing.

Chord voicings that use only the top three or four strings are used frequently in Neo-Soul, as demonstrated in this track. Practise these with palm mutes and also with the notes ringing out.

The use of open strings is very popular in gospel-style music. Bars fourteen and seventeen have chord shapes that include the open B and high E strings.

Mark was kind enough to also bounce out a backing track version of this piece, so you can play along to exactly the same thing he recorded the track to!

As well as the pieces featured in this book, make sure you check out Mark's album *Spark and Echo* for some of the grooviest and tastiest guitar playing around.

Enjoy!

Coastin' - Full Piece

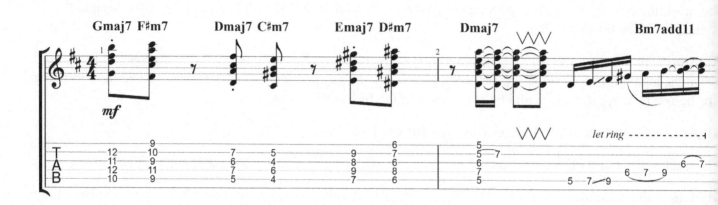

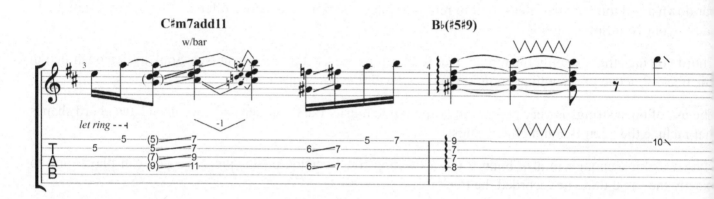

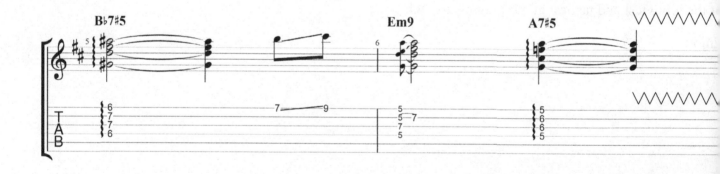

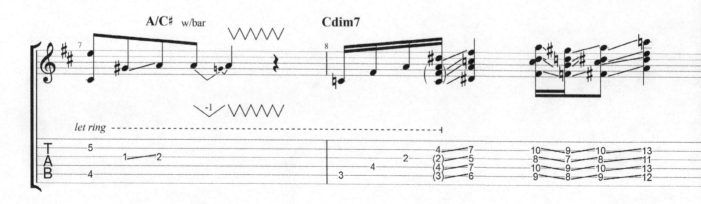

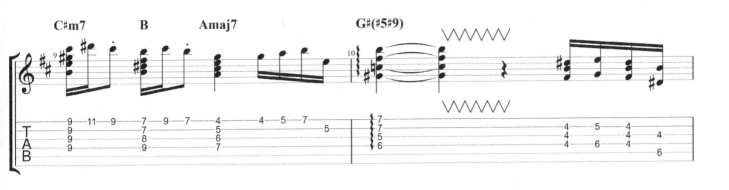

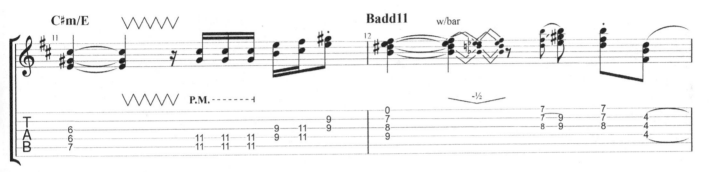

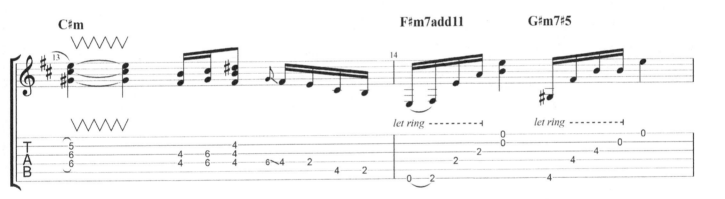

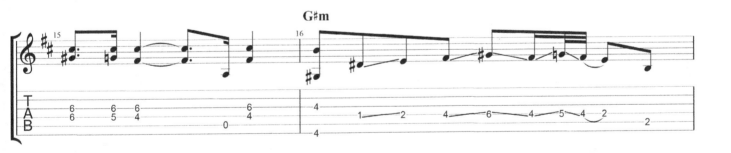

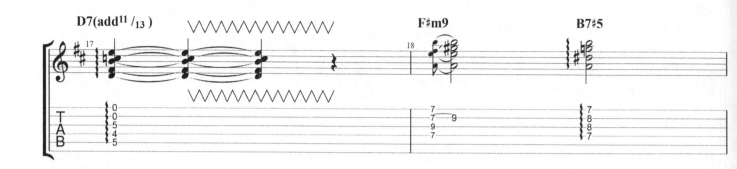

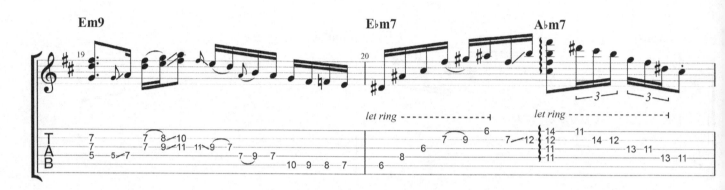

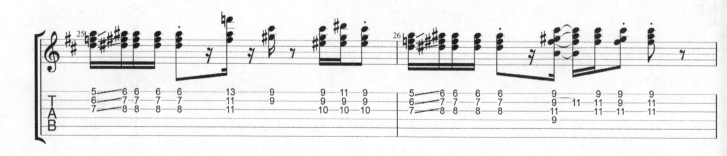

Chapter Eight – Kristof Neyens's "Fat Rat"

Fat Rat uses the B Major scale (B C# D# E F# G# A#) and includes some interesting chord voicings, single note legato lines, double-stops, artificial harmonics, and many other techniques featured in this book. The piece was written to highlight the feel of the "push and pull" of the beat that is so prominent in Neo-Soul. *Fat Rat* shows that tightness isn't always necessary to capture the Neo-Soul vibe. Make sure you watch the full video to get the feel and vibe right.

https://www.fundamental-changes.com/neo-soul-videos/

Before playing *Fat Rat,* read the tips below:

Bar two features the combination of a single note line, outlining a Bmaj9 (B D# F# A# C#) arpeggio, with a double-stop line. Aim to play this lick as smoothly and cleanly as possible before you build up speed. Smoothness is key throughout this entire piece.

Have a look at the verse of this piece. The harmonic functions are Imaj7 (Bmaj7), bVIImaj7 (Amaj7), VIm7 (G#m7), V7sus (F#7sus) and V7 (F#7). On the Amaj7 there is a single note line that ends with the Greg Howe-style vibrato we touched upon in Chapter Six.

The chorus moves from E to D#7 to G#m7. The last lick includes artificial harmonics. The harmonics are played with the pick and index finger of the picking hand, while the ring finger of the picking hand plucks the first of the fretted notes. This is followed by a pull-off by the fretting hand.

If you have worked consecutively through this book you will find the full pieces much easier to master!

To see more of Kristof's playing be sure to check out his hugely popular Instagram account below.

https://www.instagram.com/kristofneyensguitar/?hl=en

Fat Rat – Full Piece

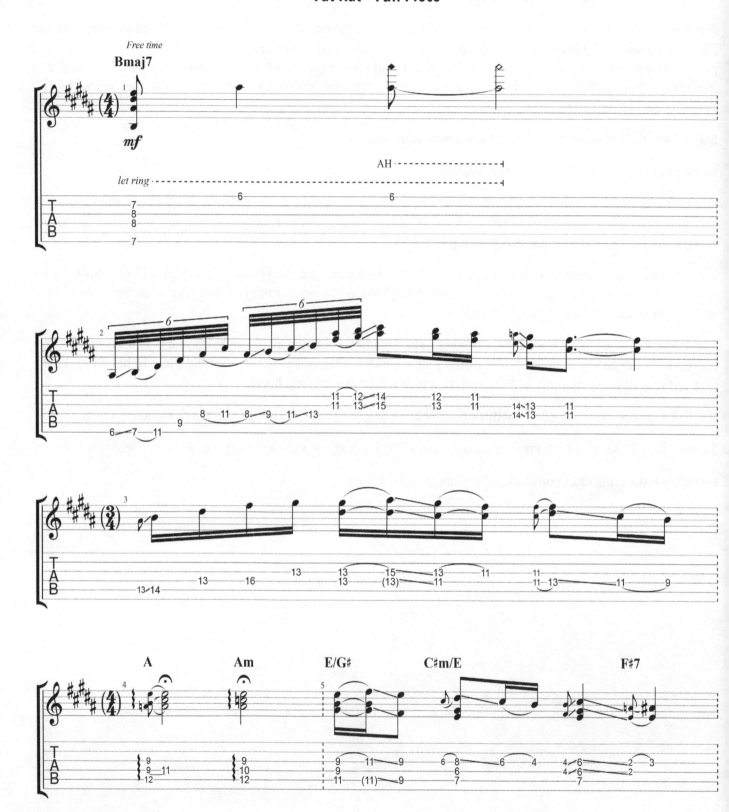

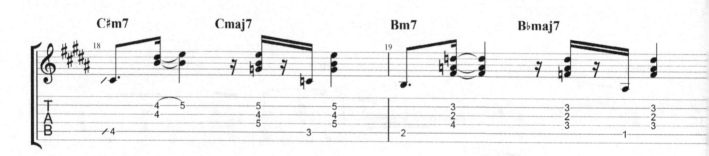

Chapter Nine – Simon Pratt's "Get Hip"

Get Hip is in the key of Eb Minor and relies heavily on the use of the Eb Minor Pentatonic scale (Eb Gb Ab Bb Db). Simon created this song to highlight the techniques of single notes, double-stops and legato chord fills. Although there are lots of embellishments in this piece, the focus always comes back to the central three chord groove of Abm11, Bbm11 and Ebm7.

We recommend watching how Simon plays this track in the accompanying video and reading the tips below before attempting this piece.

https://www.fundamental-changes.com/neo-soul-videos/

Bar one: if the notes of the double-stops are ringing out too much, add a slight palm mute.

Bars two and three: the Abm11, Bbm and Ebm7 chords featured in these bars act as the main groove for the whole piece. Make sure this pattern feels comfortable before continuing.

Bar five: pay close attention to the "let ring" and "palm muted" symbols featured in this bar.

Bar nine: learn the longer line featured in bar 9 a few notes at a time, at a tempo of around 50 bpm before speeding up.

Bars nineteen and twenty: to learn the longer single note and double-stop lick in these bars, break it down into four-note chunks and build it up bit by bit.

To see more of Simon's ideas check out his Instagram account below.

https://www.instagram.com/simeygoesfunky/

Get Hip - Full Piece

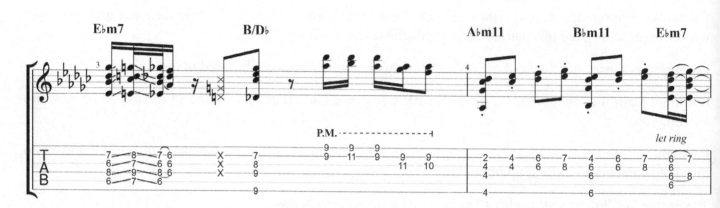

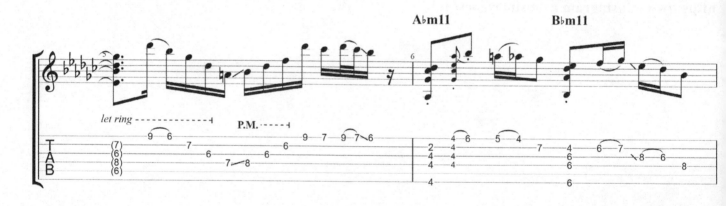

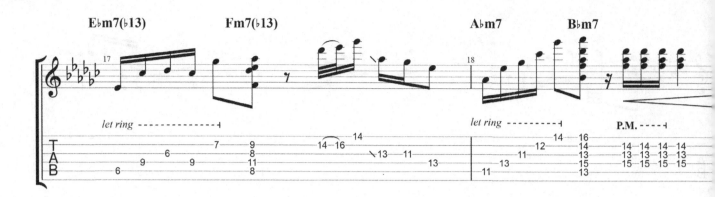

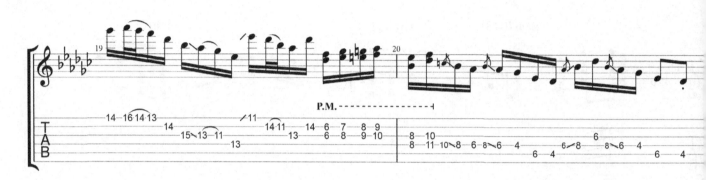

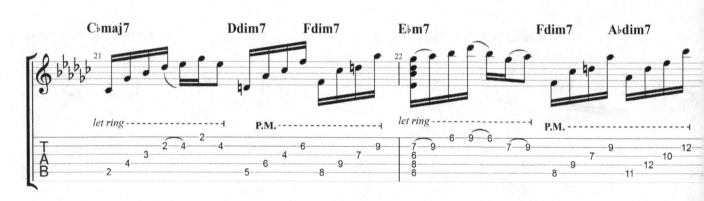

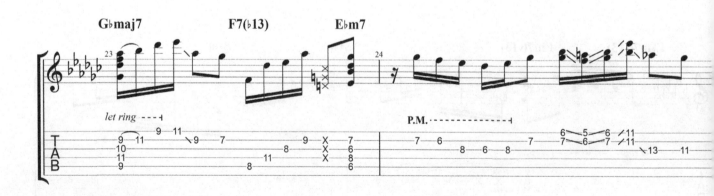

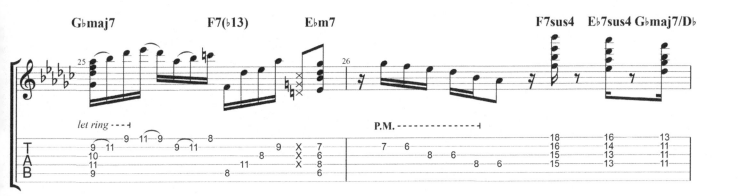

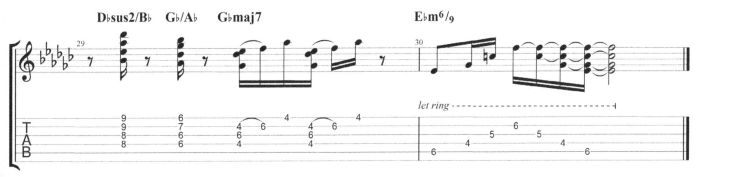

Chapter Ten – Mark Lettieri's "Sunday Brunch"

Sunday Brunch is Mark's second piece for this book. It predominantly uses the D Major scale (D E F# G A B C#), but borrows chords from related keys. As you can see in the video link below, this piece is fingerpicked.

https://www.fundamental-changes.com/neo-soul-videos/

The following tips will assist you in tackling this piece:

The piece starts with triple-stops (three notes played at the same time) where the top notes of the voicings outline a D Mixolydian scale (D E F# G A B C). Play these chords short to keep them as tight as possible. Tightness is key throughout this entire track.

Diminished chord ideas are used frequently in Neo-Soul. These chords can be useful to link progressions together, as Mark demonstrates several times in this piece (bars six, eight, eleven, thirteen, fourteen, sixteen and so on).

Look at the way chromatic approach notes and chords are used on the E7 groove, starting at bar twenty-six. There's often a movement from Eb7 to E7. Play this tight and staccato.

To check out more of Mark's incredible work, check out the links below.

https://www.instagram.com/mjlettieri/

http://bit.ly/2EhMTaZ

https://www.marklettieri.com/

Sunday Brunch – Full Piece

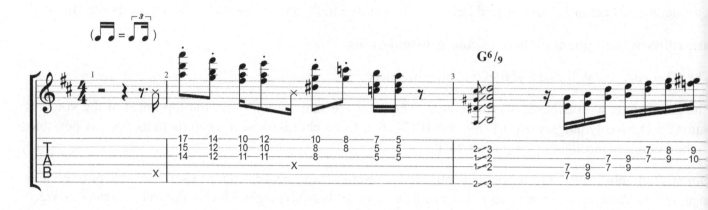

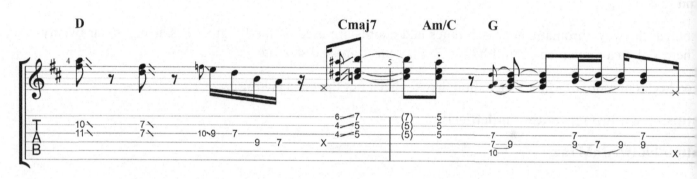

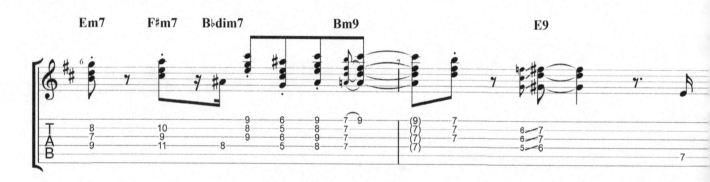

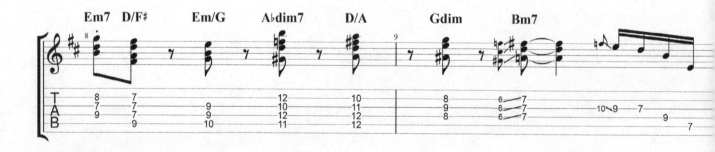

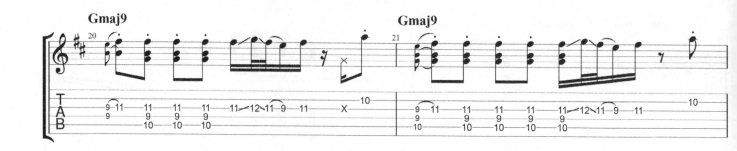

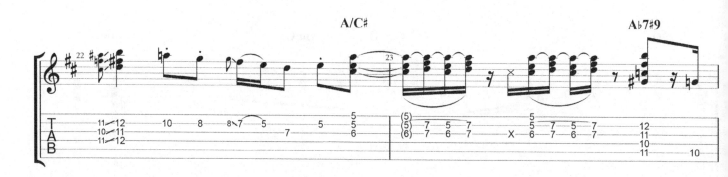

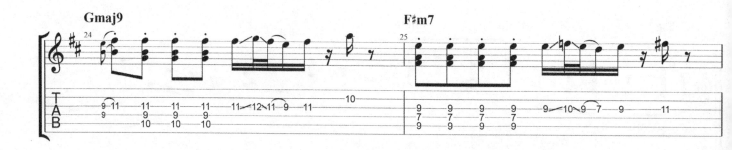

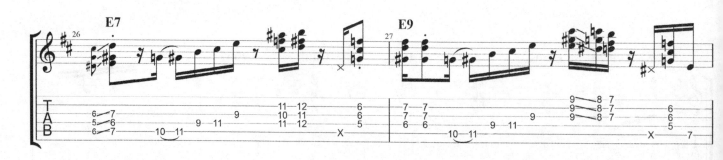

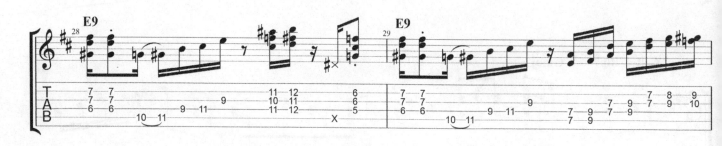

Chapter Eleven – Get the Tone

The Player

The single most important aspect of tone production is the person playing the guitar. Most profession guitarists can make any instrument or amp sound great. You are the source of tone! The first thing to do make sure that every note you play has meaning and purpose. Jeff Beck, who has recorded some of the be guitar playing on the planet, said, "Better to play one note well, than a thousand notes badly."

The Guitar

There is no specific guitar that suits playing Neo-Soul more than another, although there are some classics yo could consider:

Fender Stratocaster

Fender Telecaster

Gibson ES-335

Paul Reed Smith

These guitars and many more are all perfect for the job. Find the guitar that works best for you.

Get to know your instrument! Every instrument has subtle nuances that make it unique. Get to know how yo volume, tone and pickup selector controls can subtly shape your sound.

The pickup selector gives you control over the tone your guitar produces. The pickup nearest the bridge w have the brightest, harshest tone, and is often used for solos. The pickups produce a progressively warme smoother sound as you move towards the neck pickup. Often, people only use two of the five possible picku selector positions (on a Strat, for instance), preferring the warm neck pickup for rhythm and the bridge picku for solos and riffs. However, you should experiment with all the pickup selection options you have availabl Don't be afraid to break convention.

There are two main types of pickups: single-coil and humbucker. Single-coil pickups have a classic, clear ton They are highly dynamic and favour clean tones that cut through a mix. Humbucking pickups are warmer ar fatter sounding.

One misconception is that spending a lot of money will guarantee you an amazing instrument. Our advice to buy the best possible instrument you can afford and learn it inside out. Often, buying a second-hand guit allows you to get twice the guitar for half the money. Look online and ask your friends to see what's availabl Read reviews and be sure to search out the types of guitars used in the music you like.

The Amp

Like the guitar, there is no specific amp that is definitive when it comes to the Neo-Soul sound – although am able to produce a crystal clean tone are a good starting point. Some of our favourites include:

Fender Princeton

Fender Deluxe Reverb

Brunetti Singleman

Supro Statesman

PRS Sonzera

These days there is an enormous range of amplifiers available, so choosing one comes down to individual taste and preference.

The amplifier controls that sculpt your sound are the gain and equalisation controls. Although adjusting the gain control will influence the overall volume, think of it as a tone control, not a volume control. Adjusting the gain increases or decreases the amount of distortion heard in the amplifier. Tone creation is very personal and subjective, so listen to many different guitarists and decide what *you* want to hear, then shape the sound to your own preference.

The bass, middle and treble EQ controls on the amplifier are the main tone sculptors and allow you to mould the guitar sound to your desired tone. If you are in doubt, set your amplifier's EQ to six, five, six (bass, middle and treble respectively). This is generally a good starting point to build from and normally works when testing out a new amplifier.

For more information on amplifier controls check out:

http://bit.ly/2CH1gUE

Pedals

There aren't too many pedals needed to create the Neo-Soul sound, but investing in a good quality compressor, envelope filter and reverb would be an excellent place to start. Some of our personal favourites include:

Wampler Ego Compressor

Keeley 4 Knob Compressor

Carl Martin Classic Opto-Compressor

Electro-Harmonix Q-Tron+

Strymon Flint

Walrus Audio Fathom

Strings

The most important thing to do before any recording or live session is to re-string your guitar. We like to have had the strings on for about a day to let them settle in. Brand new strings make an incredible difference to the overall tone of the guitar. It is always amazing to see how lifeless and dull strings can get, even after a week's playing.

The lighter the strings, the easier they are to play. Heavier strings have a fatter, warmer tone, but techniques such as bending can be more challenging. Try different string gauges and manufacturers until your find a set that works for you. For the recordings in this book, Simon used Ernie Ball Super Slinky strings with a gauge of 9-42. Kristof is fond of heavier strings and used D'Addario EXL116 11-52 for his recordings.

Another important factor in tone production is how you hit the strings. The thickness of your pick/plectrum will impact your tone. The thicker the pick, the bolder and fuller the sound, whereas thinner picks will usually produce a thinner, sparkly clear tone. Simon prefers Jim Dunlop Jazz 3 plectrums – one area of his playing that has not changed over the years. He finds that the control he gets from these picks, especially when alternate picking, boosts confidence and control tremendously.

"Picks are for fairies!" is another quote from tone-master Jeff Beck! He is referring to the fact that you can get incredible control and touch by playing every note with fingers only. Most people associate finger-picking with rhythm and chord work, but finger-picked lead guitar can produce some of the most emotive and creative sounds. Put down your plectrum and play your favourite lead lines with your fingers. It is also possible to use hybrid-picking, which enables you to use both finger-picking and a pick at the same time. Kristof mostly uses hybrid-picking to achieve his sound and his current favourite pick is a Mathas Guitars Jazztor 2.0mm with beveled edges, because these picks sound great in combination with fingers.

Our Gear

Simon

Guitar: Taylor T5

Amp: Kemper using a Michael Britt Fender Tweed Profile

Recording: Logic Pro

I used my Taylor T5 (thank you Taylor), straight into my Kemper with a Michael Britt Fender Tweed Profile loaded in. I recorded each track fairly clean and dry, then added some light compression and plate reverb with Logic's Space Designer plugin.

Kristof

Guitar: Maybach Teleman T54 Vintage Cream

Effects: Carl Martin Classic Opto-Compressor; Strymon Timeline; Walrus Audio Design Monument; Strymon Flint.

Amp: Brunetti Singleman 16W combo

Recording: Sennheiser e609; Scarlett Focusrite 2i2.

I set up a fairly compressed clean sound with a little bit of plate reverb and mic'd up my amp for the examples. For *Fat Rat* I used less compression, included the Strymon Timeline for some delay, and engaged the Harmonic Tremolo of the Walrus Audio Design Monument to create a beautiful but subtle modulation.

Playing with Other Musicians

So far you have learnt licks, created fun and inspiring improvisations, and developed your tone. By working with other musicians and seeing how they create music, you will develop a better idea of how to create your own tone and style. Ask the musicians you are working with to give you constructive feedback about your tone and to pass on any ideas they may have to improve it.

Music is to be played and there is no better feeling than jamming! Our top tip for jamming with other musicians is "play with people who are better than you". Working with musicians more technically and musically advanced will inspire you. Learning to read music notation and having a good grasp of modern music theory can help you to interact with other musicians.

If you can't play with other musicians for some reason, why not invest in a looper pedal (such as the TC Electronic Ditto) to play with more of a live feel.

Backing Tracks And Drum Tracks

One thing we think is extremely important is having fun when playing! That is the thing we value most high here at Fundamental Changes. Although it is impossible for us to recreate an actual band scenario for you, w have created Neo-Soul backing and drum tracks to get as close to it as possible.

Backing Tracks

Backing Track One: Amaj7, G#7, C#m

Backing track one is based around the key of C#m and follows the three-chord progression shown above. has a classic Neo-Soul vibe in the style of J Dilla. The C#m Pentatonic scale (C# E F# G# B), the C# Blu scale (C# E F# G G# B) and the C# Natural Minor scale (C# D# E F# G# A B) are perfect choices to solo ov this progression.

Backing Track Two: Em9, Balt

Backing track two has a distinct Tom Misch flavor to it. It alternates between an Em9 chord and a variety B Altered chords, such as #5, but also a Bm9 chord too. This backing track is deliberately ambiguous and ye can use either E Minor Pentatonic (E G A B D) or B Minor Pentatonic (B D E F# A) when soloing. Experime and follow along with the melody line too.

Backing Track Three: Am7, Em7, Fmaj7

Backing track three is three-chord progression in the key of A Minor. The A Minor Pentatonic scale (A C D G), the A Blues Scale (A C D Eb E G) and the A Natural Minor scale (A B C D E F G) will work well over th progression. This track is in the style of Kerry "2 Smooth" Marshall.

Backing Track Four: E, G#m7, A6, A/B, B7b9

This backing track is taken from Example 6r. The E Major scale (E F# G# A B C# D#) works perfectly wh soloing over this example. For extra points, aim to include some natural harmonics.

Also included are backing tracks to the full songs featured in this book, so you can practise and record yours playing along to each piece.

Drum Tracks

There are a ton of examples featured in this book and while using a metronome is the most fundamental for of practice you can do, it can get a bit boring. To counteract this we have created five drum tracks at a varie of speeds for you to practise the examples shown in the book and also as a creative tool to write your own Ne Soul ideas. The drum tracks each have different feels, some with tight grooves and some with a looser feel replicate different aspects of the Neo-Soul sound.

Conclusion

Whether you are just beginning your Neo-Soul journey or you are an experienced player, we believe everyone can benefit by developing the techniques and ideas featured in this book. Use the examples as a starting point for creating your own musical lines, phrases and complete songs. Let your ears guide you and don't rely on the finger patterns and scale shapes you know to be the "safe notes'. Remember the saying, "If it sounds good it is. If it sounds bad... it probably is too!"

Practise what you don't know, not what you do! This is quite simply the best advice we can give to any musician seeking to improve.

Our passion in life is teaching people to play and express themselves through the guitar. If you have any questions, please get in touch and we will do our best to respond as quickly as possible.

You can contact us at:

simeypratt@gmail.com and,

kristof_neyens@hotmail.com

Or via the Fundamental Changes YouTube channel

Check out our Instagram Channels to see what we are up to in our own playing:

Simon : @simeygoesfunky

Kristof : @kristofneyensguitar

Other Books from Fundamental Changes

Martin Taylor
Beyond Chord Melody

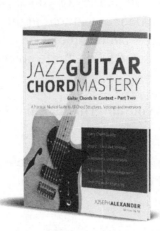

Jazz Guitar
Chord Mastery

100 Classic Jazz Licks
For Guitar

Modern Jazz
Guitar Concepts

Chord Tone Soloing
For Jazz Guitar

Complete Technique For
Modern Guitar

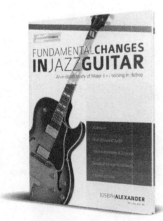

Fundamental Changes in
Jazz Guitar

Jazz Bebop
Blues Guitar

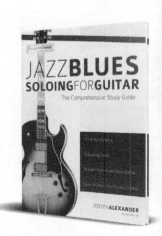

Jazz Blues Soloing
For Guitar

Made in the USA
Las Vegas, NV
19 January 2024